For Stephanie, who has been the biggest motivation
and catalyst for my own personal life change, and
loving me through my journey to true freedom.

# TABLE OF CONTENTS

# FOREWORD
## by Stephen Arterburn

Along the way, in our fallen world, outside the garden of Eden, we struggle, and we eventually get stuck. We want freedom from our habits or obsessions or wounds or addictions. We seek help and often hear perhaps the most misquoted, out of context, scripture. It comes from John 8:31,32 when people only state the phrase, "the truth will set you free." If that were true, all we would need to do is memorize scripture and we would be free. It does not work that way because the phrase, "the truth will set you free", in context does not promise freedom simply by scripture memorization or picking a particular verse to apply to a particular problem. There is much more to finding freedom. The entirety of this passage says that if you will follow the teachings of Christ, you will become a disciple of Christ. Being a disciple of Christ, by following the teachings of Christ, is what allows you to know the truth and then the truth will set you free.

The problem comes when our humanity gets in the way of following Christ. We try and fail. Then we try harder and fail harder. Some repeat this hopeless process over and over again, and nothing changes. It's called true insanity. This is why "True Freedom" is such an important book. It begins where transformation begins. Not with futile effort to create change under your own limited power, but with surrender to God who is all powerful. That is just the first of the many choices the book guides you through. Follow the directions here and by the end you will be free.

By picking up this workbook, and joining a group, you have made a great choice and taken a huge step toward true freedom. The group will provide the support you need to stay the course. Remember that awareness of a problem is better than denial, but it does not change anything. Desire for change is better than satisfaction with living in a self-constructed prison. Awareness and desire must be accompanied by willingness. Not just a one-time statement of willingness, but a daily, humble, death to self-will and surrender to God's will. Daily surrender to the path found here in "True Freedom" will lead you to be truly free.

—**Stephen Arterburn**

# FOREWORD
*by Rick Bosch*

It was 2011, and change was coming to our family. We were moving to Albuquerque, New Mexico. Up to that point, we had spent the entirety of our lives in the green Pacific Northwest. New Mexico was part of the country that I was not familiar with; in fact, I had to look at a map to see exactly where it was. What brought me down to the land of Enchantment was a position in a church helping the hurting and addicted.

It was during the springtime that we made our way south, and pretty much everything was brown as far as the eye could see. The one different thing was the blue sky; this was a welcome change from what we had known. Within days of my arrival, I started my new position, and I met Landon Porter. I immediately found out that we shared a few things in common, we were both from Washington state, and we both were fans of the Seahawks. At that time, Landon was a teacher for one of the local high schools and volunteered at our church. I immediately found that we shared another thing in common beyond living in Washington. He, too, wanted to help those that were struggling with destructive behaviors.

Landon was involved at our church for a couple of years before I started. One of his passions was helping men who struggled with sex addiction. This battle was very familiar to him because it was one that he had faced himself. He started a support group and was helping not only men from our church but also from the community. As we served alongside one another and as the program grew, it was clear that he would be the perfect fit to join me full time. Landon left his teaching job and became our group's director. Each week we would see more than 500 people looking for help and hope. Over the next several years, Landon and I developed not only a working relationship but a close friendship. During that time, I saw tremendous growth in him. He gave wise counsel to others and matured in his walk. He eventually became an ordained pastor.

Landon and I would each meet with people who struggled with addiction, anger, grief, relational pain, and many other issues. We both talked about developing a process that would not be limited to addiction but would help others with any destructive behavior.

We wanted to create something that would address the root issues and not just the outward behaviors. We wanted it to be useful for a wide range of issues. Often people believe that some things are worse than others, which is true on the outside, but inwardly they all revolve around pain. Because of this, we knew that God needed to be a part of the process. As I prayed, I sat down and began to write out a framework built around specific choices and action steps. We both believed that when you can make healthy choices, then they will move you in a positive direction. I wanted to write a book with many of my life experiences, but we needed much more than a book to help others. We needed to develop a practical workbook. It was clear to me that Landon would be the right person to write and develop it. He had spent years working with people in group environments and being a teacher; he learned what worked and what didn't. So, Landon started putting the pieces together.

When Landon finished each chapter, we wanted to make sure that we were on the right path and that it would be effective. We decided to choose four of our group leaders that had years of experience in addiction to help us with feedback. Then after making changes, we had all of our other group leaders personally go through the workbook. We heard nothing but positive comments, so we started using the material in what we call Freedom groups.

As you go through this workbook, you will find questions that will help you change how you think, bring healing, and move toward freedom. Since we have started using the True Freedom workbook, we have seen many people find healing and hope.

I don't know where you are in your life, but if you feel stuck by decisions that you have made in your past or by public or private addiction, then I believe this workbook will help you. The True Freedom workbook is designed by building a foundation and then moving into spiritual and emotional healing. What if you could make specific choices that would change your life? Would it be worth it to you? I hope you will take the journey and experience True Freedom.

—**Rick Bosch**

# ACKNOWLEDGMENTS

I want to express my appreciation for all the people who have been instrumental and supportive in my process and journey towards true freedom, and developing a principle-based curriculum to help others.

To Stephanie and my daughters, who have been patient and loving as I spent so much time writing, reading, researching and ministering to those in need of finding freedom in their lives. You have been the greatest support and encouragement to me!

To Rick Bosch, my friend, boss, partner in ministry and mentor. Words cannot express the impact you have had on my life and development as Pastor, friend, husband and father.

To Rob Wenzel, Dr. Doug Weiss, Rob McIntyre and Wesley Linam. My counselors and wisdom givers, who have helped me heal, grow and develop into a life of true freedom.

To all the leaders of Living Free at Sagebrush Church, Albuquerque, New Mexico who have served faithfully, given your time generously, and sacrificed willingly to help people through their hardest times.

To Jeff Peterson, Doug Chaplin, Richelle Wright and Keri Carmichael. As an advisory team for this project, you brought all your years of recovery experience and heart for leading others into the process of freedom, and truly made a difference in this final product.

To Jeff and Jill Petraglia, John Roberts, Scott Miller, Patricia Gonzales, Art and Marie Posey, Rick Courville, Ernie and Pat Osborne, and so many others who have served in leadership with me and helped make the Living Free ministry the best it could possibly be! Your support and lives have been like a gentle breeze or gust of wind in my sails, continually pushing me to be better!

# INTRODUCTION

Welcome to the True Freedom group workbook! We are excited that you have taken this step. We believe that the principles that you will learn over the next several weeks will be life changing. No matter what you are struggling with, these groups are designed to help you experience Freedom!

Each of us has unhealthy behaviors that can cause pain to us personally, but they can also affect those around us. These behaviors, possibly addictions or habits, can hold us back from the freedom we all desire in our lives. Freedom is the power or right to act, speak, or think, as we want without hindrance or restraint. Freedom is one of the most valuable gifts that we possess but with that freedom comes responsibility. Take for example the freedom of speech; you are free to say whatever you want to say but the person that hears you, may not be so accepting. They may be offended or hurt and because of your words a relationship may end or a job could be lost.

Think for a moment about all the choices that we make each day; the clothes that we wear, the food that we eat, the places that we go and the people that we choose to be with. Each choice makes an impact, good or bad in your life. It is said that we make the choices and then our choices make us.

As you walk through this process you will be learning 5 choices that are critical to bringing about change in your life, and freedom from the things holding you back.. Each choice is essential in building a foundation that will establish life-changing principles. As you learn these 5 choices there will be several action steps to help support each choice that you make.

I want to encourage you to focus on one day at a time. We cannot change our past and we cannot control our future but we can decide to make the right choices each day.

The decision that you made in starting this process shows that you want to make a positive change in your life. We believe that you can. Remember to never give up. You can do this and it will be worth it!

As you begin the Freedom group workbook, honesty is vital to your success. The more that you can be honest with yourself and others the more it will benefit you. You will get out of what you put into this. You may need to take time before answering some of the questions, you may need to ask others to help you remember some of your past and you may also want to pray and ask for wisdom.

Our Freedom group workbook is designed to be used along with others. Why? We need to know that we are not alone. We also need the support and encouragement of others.

It is our desire as you work through this process you will experience hope, and you will see freedom occur in your life. There is a great verse in the bible that talks about being set free. It's found in the book of John chapter 8 verse 32. *"And you will know the truth, and the truth will set you free."* I believe that as we learn the truth and apply it to our lives that we will experience true freedom.

### Group Format

Each week, your group will meet and go over the lesson in this workbook. It is imperative that you complete the work to the best of your ability, so that you can share your insights and experience. The group sharing will help everyone learn, understand and apply the principles that will help you make the choices, and take the actions, that lead to freedom!

Also, you will have a chance to briefly check-in (3-4 min each) and report out about how your week went. This is a simple accountability structure, designed to help you create habits and patterns of sharing. This structure may have been introduced in the Freedom Group Open Group, but here is what it looks like:

### Individual Check In:
1. How long have you been free/sober? (how many days, weeks, months, or years?)
2. Did you maintain the recovery principles this week? (Sun Mon Tue Wed Thu Fri Sat)
   - Pray in the Morning: _____ days
   - Read: Bible _____ days / recovery materials _____ days
   - Call or Contact someone: _____ days
   - Meetings: _____meetings (includes church, AA meetings, other group)
   - Pray in the Evening: _____ days

3. What did you learn from your recovery work this week?
4. What was your greatest struggle or victory this week?
5. Are you open to feedback?

## Explanation of Check-In

1. This is your opportunity to report out on your progress towards sobriety or freedom from your struggle or destructive habit. This can be helpful for encouragement, a chance to develop honesty and solicit support from the group.

2. There are Five Recovery Principles that you can commit to each day of each week. These principles are building the foundation of structure and change in your life, and can be completed each day in a short amount of time. Small, consistent changes build better, longer lasting habits and lead to life change!

    **Morning Prayer:** This is a chance to start your day in simple prayer.

    **Read:** It is helpful to begin the habit of reading your Bible and Recovery Material each day. There are many helpful recovery or non-fiction books about many of the struggles you may face.

    **Call or Contact:** It is always good to make a phone call each day to someone in the group, or in your support circle. Maintaining contact throughout the week helps build trust and provides healthy accountability.

    **Meetings:** It is good to attend other meetings or groups to help support your recovery or life change process. This could include other recovery groups, counseling sessions, Bible study groups, church attendance or any meeting where you are encouraged towards your growth.

    **Evening Prayer:** This is a chance to end each day with a simple prayer. This could be focused on gratitude, repentance or honest confession.

3. This is your chance to share what you learned from the work you completed this past week. You can also share what you learned from your readings, Bible study, or counseling.

4. This is an opportunity to share with the group what your biggest struggle or temptation may have been in the last week. You can also report on your victories, big or small!

5. This gives the group a chance to share feedback with you, which may include encouragement, challenges or support. You have the choice and freedom to solicit feedback, or to decline for each meeting depending on your own self-awareness and your level of openness to receiving the feedback.

# THE CHOICE OF SURRENDER

*Action 1—Doing Whatever it takes to Change*

Somewhere, deep within all of us, we know what it is. Perhaps we haven't said it aloud, but that doesn't mean it doesn't exist. It is something you are ready to be done with, something that has caused damage, and something that you can't change on your own. You are ready to be free from it, and today is the day to start.

The first step to freedom is to admit that you need to change. It is time to admit that the real source of your problems is you, which means that you are also a part of the solution. You have amazing potential to partner with God to change your life!

Why do you want to change?

_____
_____
_____
_____
_____

To "admit" means to acknowledge what is already a known fact. As you seek freedom, you will need to be brave and admit to yourself that there is something that you need to change.

What is "it"? What are you ready to be free from? What are the destructive habits or patterns in your life that are holding you back from the freedom you desire?

Take some time to pray and reflect on the following list of problems that you may have in your life, and to what degree do you struggle with them. On a scale of 1-5, with 5 being the greatest degree of struggle, circle the degree of struggle:

| Symptom/Behavior | Degree of Struggle | | | | |
|---|---|---|---|---|---|
| Alcohol | 1 | 2 | 3 | 4 | 5 |
| Anger | 1 | 2 | 3 | 4 | 5 |
| Anxiety/Fear | 1 | 2 | 3 | 4 | 5 |
| Compulsive spending | 1 | 2 | 3 | 4 | 5 |
| Control Issues | 1 | 2 | 3 | 4 | 5 |
| Cutting/Self-harm | 1 | 2 | 3 | 4 | 5 |
| Drugs | 1 | 2 | 3 | 4 | 5 |
| Food/Overeating | 1 | 2 | 3 | 4 | 5 |
| Gambling | 1 | 2 | 3 | 4 | 5 |
| Internet Over-use | 1 | 2 | 3 | 4 | 5 |
| Lying | 1 | 2 | 3 | 4 | 5 |
| Overworking/workaholic | 1 | 2 | 3 | 4 | 5 |
| Pornography/Sexual Purity | 1 | 2 | 3 | 4 | 5 |
| Prescription Drugs | 1 | 2 | 3 | 4 | 5 |
| Rebellion | 1 | 2 | 3 | 4 | 5 |
| Relationships | 1 | 2 | 3 | 4 | 5 |
| Smoking | 1 | 2 | 3 | 4 | 5 |
| Stealing | 1 | 2 | 3 | 4 | 5 |
| Video Games | 1 | 2 | 3 | 4 | 5 |
| Other: | 1 | 2 | 3 | 4 | 5 |
| Other: | 1 | 2 | 3 | 4 | 5 |

What are the three strongest symptoms/behaviors you circled?

1. _____

2. _____

3. _____

Which one of these do you want to focus on to gain freedom from?

_____

_____

_____

_____

_____

Admitting your problems is probably one of the hardest things you will ever do! What are some of the feelings you are having about admitting?

_____

_____

_____

_____

_____

What has been a roadblock or something that has kept you from admitting you have these struggles and need a change?

_____

_____

_____

_____

_____

Why haven't you done anything about it earlier? If you have, why didn't you change?

_____

_____

_____

_____

_____

How does your struggle or destructive habit affect your behaviors, thoughts and emotions?

_____

_____

_____

_____

_____

How does your struggle or destructive habit affect your relationships?

_____

_____

_____

_____

_____

How does your struggle or destructive habit keep you safe or protect you from being vulnerable or hurt?

_____

_____

_____

_____

_____

In order to change, you need others to help and support you. Who can help you through this process?

_____

_____

_____

_____

_____

Six months from now, what do you hope your life will look like?

_____

_____

_____

_____

_____

# THE CHOICE OF SURRENDER

*Action 2—Identify the Consequences of My Behavior*

Now that you have admitted your struggle, habit or destructive pattern of behavior in your life, it's time for an honest look at the results. What has happened because of your actions? What are the true consequences of your choices?

In many ways, your destructive patterns or addictions, may have served you well over the years, giving pleasure or relief, comforting you from troubles, or medicating the pains or struggles in life. Yet, because of these behaviors, you have experienced results or consequences, both positive and negative, in many different ways. In some ways, your struggle or addiction has been helpful and given you satisfaction or comfort.

What has your struggle, destructive behavior or addiction given you?

_____
_____
_____
_____
_____

How has your behavior in your struggles helped you cope with life?

_____
_____

_____

_____

_____

Your behaviors and choices also impact those around you, possibly in negative ways, with undesirable or unfortunate consequences.

Have you observed your behaviors with your struggle, destructive pattern or addiction making a negative impact on other people in your life? YES / NO

Who has it impacted and what was the effect?

_____

_____

_____

_____

_____

Our destructive patterns, struggles, or addictions have caused damage and chaos in several areas of our lives. The results of those actions and behaviors have a more widespread impact than we want to believe.

How have destructive patterns, struggles or addictions impacted theses various areas of your life?

**Marriage**

_____

_____

_____

_____

_____

**Job or Work**

_____

_____

_____

_____

_____

**Relationships**

_____

_____

_____

_____

_____

_____

**Self-worth**

_____

_____

_____

_____

_____

_____

Looking at the consequences of our actions and behaviors can be sobering and emotional. What feelings do you have about listing the effects of our struggles, destructive patterns and addictions?

_____

_____

_____

_____

_____

_____

How have your destructive pattern, struggle or addiction led you to compromise your beliefs, values, convictions and principles?

_____

_____

_____

_____

_____

_____

How would life look and feel without your destructive pattern, struggle or addiction, and the results of those behaviors?

_____

_____

_____

_____

_____

_____

# THE CHOICE OF SURRENDER

*Action 3—Finding Help Outside of Myself*

.

Sometimes the consequences of our actions and behaviors can be overwhelming and actually seem unmanageable or out of control. Most people don't like the feeling of being out of control. It is usually scary when you lose control of your car or your boat and the result of losing control is usually not a positive ending. Most people equate control with authority, strength, or force. The lack of these is not what most of us desire. In fact, many of us work hard to control ourselves and everyone else in our lives. When we fail at control, we feel like failures or "less than".

What are things you have control over in your life?

_____

_____

_____

_____

_____

What are things you ***don't*** have control over in life?

_____

_____

_____

_____

_____

_____

If we really want change in our lives and gain freedom from the struggles, destructive patterns, and addictions then we have to surrender and face our pain and chaos head on. This requires a decision to face reality and admit that our life isn't working with us in control, but we are out of control. Many people feel this lack of control is a weakness or flaw, yet we can change and see our powerlessness as a strength and chance for positive change.

This means that we need to admit we are powerless, that we cannot control it. We have no authority, strength or power to stop our destructive thoughts, patterns or behaviors. And we need to find help outside of ourselves.

What evidence in your life points to your lack of control or powerlessness?

_____

_____

_____

_____

_____

_____

How does it make you feel to see how your struggles, behaviors, and addictions are out of control?

_____

_____

_____

_____

_____

_____

In many ways, our struggles and behavior patterns could be considered "insane". A common working definition of insanity is "continuing to do the same things, over and over, expecting a different result." How many of us can relate to that feeling? We have tried the same thing, over and over with more intensity and more effort, yet without the desired result.

How have you tried to stop or change in the past? What was the result?

_____

_____

_____

_____

_____

What would it take to make your problem painful enough that you would change?

_____

_____

_____

_____

_____

Change is not a natural or easy task for anyone. Yet, you may have believed that change is easy as 1-2-3 or perhaps you thought, "I will just stop." Many people have thought this and tried, but have been unsuccessful. There is truth to the statement, "if you could have stopped, then you would have already stopped." If you could have made the change, then you would have already made the change in your life. But if the evidence points to a need for change, then what will it take to make that change? If you have unsuccessfully tried to change by yourself, then it is time to seek, find and get help in this process.

Who or what can help you make the change you desire?

_____

_____

_____

_____

_____

What is your biggest obstacle to asking for help or allowing someone to help you make the change in your life?

_____

_____

_____

_____

Who is someone (excluding your spouse) you know that is healthy in your area of struggle or may have already made similar changes that could help you in this process?

_____

_____

_____

_____

_____

# THE CHOICE OF SURRENDER
*Action 4—Submit to Christ*

Last time we talked about admitting that we can't fix ourselves because we have tried unsuccessfully many times before. So what do we do? Well, we need help. That is what this choice is all about.

***Surrender*** means to give up control. We are going to look at giving up our control to someone that can help us experience freedom. Most of us have a sense that there is a God; that He is all-powerful and perfect. Most of us also understand that the world we live in is sinful and messed up. Let's look at a verse that will clarify this.

> *"For the wages of sin is death, but the free gift of*
> *God is eternal life through Christ Jesus our Lord."*
> —Romans 6:23 (NLT)

Sin is not living up to God's standards; literally, it means "missing the mark". It means that we have all done things that we shouldn't have done.

What are some things that you have done in your life that you know God wouldn't approved of?

_____

_____

_____

_____

_____

The verse explains the wages of sin. Wages are something that we have earned. What have we earned from our sin?

_____

_____

_____

_____

_____

Now there is an important word in this verse and it is "but". Go ahead and circle the word "but". That word indicates a contrast between the beginning and end of that verse— ***"but the free gift of God is eternal life through Christ Jesus our Lord."***

So, in contrast to the consequences of your sinful actions being spiritual death, God offers a free gift of eternal life. If I were to offer you a free gift, let's say a free pen or some candy, what would have to happen for it to be a free gift for you? You would have to accept it, right? In other words, if you don't take the gift I offer, then it is just a "potentially" free gift that you haven't' received yet.

What is the "potentially" free gift God is offering you?

_____

_____

_____

_____

_____

So, there is a gap between us and God, the question is, how can we receive this free gift? It comes through Jesus Christ and what He did by dying on the cross. Jesus came to this earth as a perfect man and He died on a cross to pay or to make payment for our sins. Through Jesus Christ we can have eternal life.

This also explained in another scripture, John 3:16.

> *"For this is how God loved the world: He gave His one and only Son, so that everyone who believes in Him will not perish but have eternal life."*
> —John 3:16 (NLT)

This verse demonstrates how God paid for, gives you, the free gift, but according to this scripture, what do you have to do to receive it?

_____

_____

_____

_____

_____

Can we bridge that gap between ourselves and God? YES / NO

Have you tried to bridge that gap in the past? What did you try and how did that work out for you?

_____

_____

_____

_____

_____

Are you willing to receive the free gift that God is offering? YES / NO

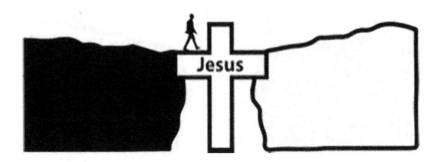

In order to receive the free gift from God, you can simply follow the A, B, C's:

**Admit**—You need to admit that you are a sinner, and that you have done things against God and you created the gap between you and God. (Romans 3:23)

**Believe**—You believe that Jesus died as payment for your sins and that God raised Him back to life, defeating death. This belief is more than just saying words, it is placing your full weight and trust in the truth of who God is and what He has done for you.

**Commit**—You commit your life by giving God *control* of your life, and you surrender to His authority. It's an act of giving Him the keys to your life, and allowing Him to control and create the change you need.

If you are ready to accept Christ as your free gift, and trust that He will bring freedom from your struggles, addictions and destructive patterns, then take a moment to pray this prayer or something similar, just follow the A, B, C's. You can use the space provided to write out your own confession and commitment to follow Christ.

*Dear Lord, I come to You admitting that I am a sinner, and I have done things against Your will. I believe that You sent Your son Jesus to die on the cross for my sins and pay my penalty, and that He rose again, defeating the grave and death. I commit my life to You, choosing to follow You, trust You and give You control of my life. Thank You Lord! In Jesus' name, Amen.*

_____

_____

_____

_____

_____

The bible says, *"For I can do everything through Christ, who gives me strength."*
—Philippians 4:13 (NLT)

How can accepting Christ and believing in God help you create the life change and freedom you are seeking from your struggles, addictions, and destructive patterns?

_____

_____

_____

_____

_____

This week, tell someone about the decision that you made. Write their name on the line below:

_____

_____

_____

_____

_____

# THE CHOICE OF SURRENDER

*Action 5—Surrender Daily*

The choice to trust Jesus brings about a whole new perspective to the process of changing and gaining freedom in your life. But the choice is not just a one-time decision with only a momentary effect on your life. It will need to become a daily decision. The good news is that Jesus wants to help you and provide the power and strength daily, to make changes that you, under your own willpower, have not been able to make. The decision to trust Jesus requires daily attention and surrender.

At the end of most military conflicts, there is one side of the conflict that has to surrender to the other side. Two armies may have been battling for months or years until one side recognizes the certain defeat. In order to save lives, they decide to surrender. Keep in mind that when the surrendering army surrenders, they don't change their minds the next day and continue fighting! Unlike a military campaign, surrendering when walking with Jesus is not a one-time event. The act of surrender becomes a daily decision and has lasting, and on-going effects, each and every day thereafter.

The same is true when you decide to surrender your life and control to God. It is truly a daily, sometimes hourly choice to surrender, not just a once-in-a-life decision. Just like the end to military conflicts, if we choose not to surrender, then there are usually certain disastrous results. When you choose to surrender to God, the results are not disastrous, but victorious. This type of surrender brings freedom each and every day that we make the decision.

*Jesus said, **"If any of you wants to be My follower, you must turn from your selfish ways, take up your cross daily, and follow Me"***
—Luke 9:23 (NLT)

What selfish ways do you need to give up? What does taking up your cross daily mean to you?

_____

_____

_____

_____

_____

Humans are creatures of habit. The many decisions we make every day determine our way of life—each decision makes us who we are.

What are some of the biggest decisions you make on a daily basis? How does this affect your life?

_____

_____

_____

_____

_____

What decisions would indicate your daily choice to surrender?

_____

_____

_____

_____

_____

There are several areas we could categorize for choices of surrender in our lives. These areas include words, attitude, thoughts, actions, and relationships. For each area, write down what you could do to surrender daily:

## Surrendering your words

> *"The words of the godly are a life-giving fountain;*
> *the words of the wicked conceal violent intentions."*
> —Proverbs 10:11 (NLT)

_____

_____

_____

_____

_____

## Surrendering your attitude

> *"You must have the same attitude that Christ Jesus had."*
> —Philippians 2:5 (NLT)

_____

_____

_____

_____

_____

## Surrendering your thoughts

> *"We demolish arguments and every pretension that sets itself up against the*
> *knowledge of God, and we take captive every thought to make it obedient to Christ."*
> —2 Corinthians 10:5 (NIV)

_____

_____

_____

_____

_____

## Surrendering your actions

> *"Our actions will show that we belong to the truth,*
> *so we will be confident when we stand before God."*
> —1 John 3:19 (NLT)

_____

_____

_____

_____

_____

_____

## Surrender your relationships

> *"Don't be fooled by those who say such things,*
> *for "bad company corrupts good character."*
> —1 Corinthians 15:33 (NLT)

_____

_____

_____

_____

_____

_____

In which area (words, attitude, thoughts, actions, and relationships) do you struggle the most? Why is this area a struggle?

_____

_____

_____

_____

_____

_____

What or who would be obstacles or road blocks to making these daily surrenders?

_____

_____

_____

_____

_____

Who can help you as you make these choices to surrender each day?

_____

_____

_____

_____

As you daily surrender your life to Christ, you must be willing to make sacrifices and deny yourself. Kyle Idleman, in his book ***Not a Fan***, says this: "You won't be able to take the path of following Jesus without walking away from a different path." This means we must be intentional to make wise decisions that represent our surrender to Jesus Christ.

This means you choose to follow Jesus, completely. You choose Jesus over the world and culture around you. You choose Jesus over the pursuit of money and career success. You choose Jesus over getting drunk or high. You choose Jesus over pornography or the affair. You choose Jesus over the new car or bigger, nicer house. You choose Jesus over what others may think of you. You choose Jesus over controlling others with anger or manipulation. You choose Jesus in every circumstance. Completely and daily.

This may sound like a difficult task, but it starts with one decision and one choice. One builds on another, and pretty soon you are surrendering and choosing Jesus daily.

# THE CHOICE OF OWNERSHIP
*Action 1—Take Responsibility*

Do you remember when you bought your first car? You were probably so excited to get the keys and drive it around town, and show all your friends. And pretty soon, you realized the car didn't run without gas, so you had to plan and pay for regularly filling up. Then, you realized the car would need an oil change, and possibly a tune-up. And perhaps you had that moment when you heard a "clunk" and you had a feeling something wasn't right in the engine, and that may have meant several hundred dollars in repairs. That is a great example of ownership. The car was yours, but so were repairs and the maintenance.

The same is true for your life. You must take ownership of your life, which includes taking responsibility for all the things related to where you are today. This means that you must understand how your choices have led you to this moment, and how the circumstances and situations in your life all play a part in the journey to get to this moment. And, if you are not satisfied with where you are—then you have to take the proper responsibility for the actions that led you here.

Taking responsibility for your actions or failures can be very difficult, and is not something that is natural or usually well taught growing up. Sometimes we can believe that taking responsibility will only bring guilt and shame to our lives. Remember that God does not base his love and acceptance for us on what we have done. His love is unconditional. Taking responsibility is just being honest with ourselves.

Why is it so difficult to look at your own life and take responsibility?

_____

_____

_____

_____

_____

_____

_____

What consequences have you experienced from not taking responsibility?

_____

_____

_____

_____

_____

_____

_____

Often, people tend to avoid taking responsibility by playing the victim, turning responsibility away from themselves, and deflecting it onto someone else.

In what ways have you avoided taking responsibility for your life, your choices and circumstances?

_____

_____

_____

_____

_____

_____

_____

There are several different patterns of behavior that prevent people from looking at themselves and taking responsibility. Let's look at some of these and see how you have experienced any of these obstacles:

## Denial

This is actively denying the reality of the problem (I don't have an anger problem, I am not addicted, I am doing fine)

How have you denied responsibility for your problem and avoided taking responsibility for the consequences, behaviors or circumstances surrounding your struggle?

_____

_____

_____

_____

_____

_____

## Excuses

Making excuses is actively finding half-truths, lies or shifting the blame so that you can avoid taking responsibility for the struggle or problem. (I have been going through a lot of stress, I just did it to have fun, etc.)

What type of excuses have you made to avoid taking responsibility?

_____

_____

_____

_____

_____

_____

## Minimize

We often minimize the struggle and issue, rather than face the reality or responsibility for it. (It's not that big of a problem, It's just a bump in the road, etc.)

How have you minimized the struggle or issue, in order to avoid taking responsibility?

_____

_____

_____

_____

_____

## Comparison

People sometimes make comparisons with others as a way to avoid responsibility and make them look better and feel better about their actions or struggles. (I'm not as bad as my boss or my dad or my old girlfriend, etc.) Who have you compared yourself too and how have you compared your behaviors to others?

_____

_____

_____

_____

_____

## Justify

People will justify their actions and behavior, in order to rationalize and gain approval for the mistakes or circumstances they created. (I only did it to relieve some tension, I did it because everyone else there was doing it, I'm just hurting from the divorce)

How have you justified your behaviors or actions, in order to avoid responsibility?

_____

_____

_____

_____

_____

There may be many reasons why you have avoided taking responsibility, and there are many reasons that you have done what you did. But, if you truly want freedom from the struggle or destructive behavior patterns, then you must be willing to take responsibility.

Galatians 6:5 says "for we are each responsible for our own conduct." And 2 Corinthians 5:10 states "for we must all stand before Christ to be judged. We will each receive whatever we deserve for the good or evil we have done in this earthly body." How can these two scriptures help direct you toward taking responsibility?

_____

_____

_____

_____

_____

# THE CHOICE OF OWNERSHIP
## Action 2—Personal Assessment Part 1

Now is the time to take a personal assessment of your life and begin the process of taking responsibility and ownership of the struggles, behaviors and circumstances that have led you to this point. Everyone has done things that we shouldn't have done, and these actions have caused others and ourselves pain. And everyone has experienced pain caused by the actions and behavior of others and that has impacted our life. But as you look at your experiences in an honest and transparent way, then you can begin to take ownership. This will help you see an overall picture of your life, so that you can move forward toward healing, life change and freedom.

This personal assessment will take a balanced approach to the past, looking at your "good", "bad" and "ugly". The **"good"** are the positive things that have happened or you have done. Be sure to identify positive events or strengths in your life, such as career advancements and achievements. The **"bad"** are the negative things that have happened or you have done. Be sure to consider significant losses in life, which could include harm that was done to you, or harm you may have caused to others.

There will also be things that happened to you that you weren't responsible for, such as car accidents, surgeries, parent's divorce, abuse or neglect, which could be considered the **"ugly"** part of life.

*"Search me, God, and know my heart;*
*test me and know my anxious thoughts."*
—Psalm 139:23

The good news about this personal assessment is that you won't do it alone. God will be with you during the whole process, and will help to reveal what you need to see and gain self-awareness.

How can shame or guilt keep you from being honest and moving forward in your personal assessment?

_____

_____

_____

_____

_____

Example:

| Season of Life | Good | Bad | Ugly |
|---|---|---|---|
| **Childhood** | won a spelling bee <br> made all-star team | took first drink <br> bullied by neighbor | parent's divorce |
| **Young Adult** | Graduated college | stole pornography <br> started partying | victim in car accident |

## CHILDHOOD

**Good**

**Bad**

**Ugly**

*YOUNG ADULT*

**Good**

**Bad**

**Ugly**

## *ADULTHOOD*

| Good |
| --- |
| |

| Bad |
| --- |
| |

| Ugly |
| --- |
| |

It is a natural tendency to avoid looking or dealing with the past and moving on, but you must look at the past in order to move forward. The importance of this personal assessment is not to feel like you are a failure, but rather to help you take ownership of your life. Remember, God does not condemn you, but he gives you freedom through the power of the Holy Spirit. And remember that this is our goal, freedom.

> *"So now there is no condemnation for those who belong to Christ Jesus. And because you belong to him, the power of the life-giving Spirit has freed you from the power of sin that leads to death."*
> —Romans 8:1-2

How does this verse give you encouragement moving forward toward freedom?

_____

_____

_____

_____

_____

# THE CHOICE OF OWNERSHIP
## Action 2—Personal Assessment Part 2

As we continue taking a personal assessment it is important to acknowledge the positive and negative experiences and behaviors that have impacted your life. You can see how various circumstances and consequences have played a role in your inability to overcome the struggle or addiction in your life.

Dr. James Reeves, Pastor of City on a Hill Church in Dallas/Fort Worth, states "about 2% of life is circumstances, and the rest of it is consequences from the choices that I've made." This means that you have no control or responsibility for the circumstances of your life, but you can take full responsibility for the consequences of your choices, or actions in life.

This is actually a beautiful thing because if we can take responsibility for the negative choices we have made, then it means that we can also take responsibility for the positive choices that we can make, and these can result in more positive outcomes in recovery. God works in us and through us, as we surrender our will to His will and He can give us strength to make the positive choices, which He can use to bring a positive outcome in our life.

Which consequences from your past negative choices are you still dealing with today? How can you face the consequences with God's help?

_____

_____

_____

_____

_____

It is also important to take assessment of your strengths and weaknesses in various relationships and different areas of life. These have played an important role in how you view others and operate in your life. Take some time to pray and consider the following relationships and areas of your life, and acknowledge the strength and weakness of each one.

Example:

| Area to Evaluate | Strengths | Weaknesses |
|---|---|---|
| **My Father** | Companionship<br>Respectful<br>Common interests and quality time | Lack of meaningful communication<br>Lack of boundaries<br>Never measure up |

| Area to Evaluate | Strengths | Weaknesses |
|---|---|---|
| **Relationship with Mother** | | |
| **Relationship with Father** | | |
| **Marriage / Singleness** | | |

| Area to Evaluate | Strengths | Weaknesses |
|---|---|---|
| Friendships | | |
| Work/Job | | |
| Financial | | |
| Dealing with Authorities | | |

| Area to Evaluate | Strengths | Weaknesses |
|---|---|---|
| Spiritual | | |

After completing the personal assessment of the different areas of your life, can you identify any common themes or patterns?

_____

_____

_____

_____

_____

_____

Which of the identified weaknesses could be an obstacle to moving forward? And why?

_____

_____

_____

_____

_____

Which of the identified strengths could be beneficial and most impactful to moving forward? And why?

_____

_____

_____

_____

Haggai 1:7 says, ***"This is what the Lord Almighty says: "Give careful thought to your ways."***

Proverbs 4:26 says, ***"Give careful thought to the paths for your feet and be steadfast in all your ways."***

How can the instruction from these two scriptures be helpful as you find freedom from your struggles, habits and addictions?

_____

_____

_____

_____

_____

# THE CHOICE OF OWNERSHIP
*Action 3—Identify Attachments*

One of the benefits from taking a personal assessment is the perspective gained on your life. You cannot live today in denial from what happened in your past, but you can use the lessons from your past to inform and shape your future. As you have seen, there are events and patterns that have shaped who you are today.

What are the top 5 events that have shaped your life—positive or negative?

1. _____

_____

2. _____

_____

3. _____

_____

4. _____

_____

5. _____

_____

During your experiences and development, you have created attachments that may be healthy and unhealthy, helpful or harmful and productive or destructive. When you attach to something that is unhealthy you give it power and control over you, and that gives you a sense of safety or satisfaction. Every attachment is an attempt to meet an unmet need in your life, but the unhealthy attachments cannot give you what you are looking for or set you free. Only God can do that.

The bible says that anything that we look to for satisfaction, outside of God, is an idol. ***"You must not make for yourself an idol of any kind or an image of anything in the heavens or on the earth or in the sea."*** Exodus 20:4

This is why it is important to identify the attachments in our life, and acknowledge how it has controlled your life and affected your relationships.

***Desires*** are anything you use to cope, escape to, seek comfort in, gain control, meet your needs or have your identity in. We must evaluate how our desires have created unhealthy attachments and their affect on our life.

What you do in life comes out of who are as a person, and what you are attached to. When you attach yourself to the things you desire, and focus your attention and energy to fulfill those desires, then you give power to them and allow them to control you.

Here a few common desires that can create unhealthy attachments. Record how they may have controlled you and affected your life:

*(You may need more space, feel free to write more in a journal or on notepad)*

| Desire | How it controls me: | How it affects my relationships/life: |
| --- | --- | --- |
| Example: Body Image | It affects my self worth, fear, comparison | Insecure, superficial |
| MONEY/STATUS | | |
| BODY IMAGE | | |
| DRUGS & ALCOHOL | | |
| RELATIONSHIPS | | |

| | | |
|---|---|---|
| WORK/SCHOOL | | |
| FOOD | | |
| POSSESSIONS | | |
| SEX | | |
| BEING NEEDED | | |
| ATTENTION | | |
| ACHIEVEMENT | | |
| Other: | | |
| Other: | | |

In whatever area(s) you struggle with, how have these attachments affected you?

_____

_____

_____

_____

_____

Now, let's begin the process of detaching from these attachments. Make a list of the attachments you are willing and need to give up and explain what life will look like without the unhealthy attachment. Then look for scripture promises from God to help you replace that attachment, and put the focus and attention back on God meeting the need in your life.

| Attachment | Life without it ... | Scripture Promises |
|---|---|---|
| Example: Money | Free from worry and stress, more generous | Matt. 6:19 *"Do not store up for yourselves treasures on earth"* |
| | | |
| | | |
| | | |
| | | |
| | | |

# THE CHOICE OF OWNERSHIP
### Action 4—Practice Transparency

The next step in your journey toward freedom and healing comes from embracing and practicing transparency. That is a scary word for many people. Transparency requires a willingness to be vulnerable and share your life, the real truth of our life, to someone else. Most people experience fear when attempting to open up and be honest with their past.

What are some of the fears you have about telling the truth of your past to another person?

_____

_____

_____

_____

_____

_____

You may have been hurt in the past when you were honest or vulnerable, so your natural instinct is to hide or create a mask. You may have believed that you can present an image of yourself that seems more presentable or acceptable to others. But in the end, the mask or image falls short and empty, and you realize that your mask cannot experience the love and freedom of Christ.

Instead, you try to manipulate, lie and manage your persona, so that no one really knows the truth of your life. And in many ways, this has kept you safe from judgment or ridicule. But it has also kept you isolated and stuck in your own struggles, addictions or unhealthy patterns of life.

What would the best possible outcome of you taking off your mask?

_____

_____

_____

_____

_____

Transparency in action will require you to admit your wrongs of the past, and be truthful about the decisions and mistakes you have made. And when you admit these to someone else, you may experience guilt, shame and fear, which are the product of pride or ego, and can eventually block the possibility for spiritual growth and life change.

What are your feelings that may hold you back from completely honest?

_____

_____

_____

_____

_____

As you embrace transparency, you must consider the people you will trust with your true self and your past. Developing trust in relationships takes courage, but with the help of God, you can trust the right people. This type of trust in other people begins with trusting God, and believing that He is good and wants the best for you. Then, you can begin to trust another person, because you will know that God will protect you and be there for you every step of the way.

Who are three people you can trust to share your personal assessment with?

1. _____

2. _____

3. _____

Now is the time to take that next step and practice transparency. Take the time to call someone, or meet them for coffee or lunch. Set up a time to sit down and talk with the person you trust and share with them what you have been learning. Share with them the good, bad and ugly, as well as the personal strengths and weaknesses, from your personal assessment.

After you have shared with that other person, write down what the experience was like:

_____

_____

_____

_____

_____

How have you experienced freedom from this choice to take ownership of your life, taking personal assessment, and then sharing that with another person?

_____

_____

_____

_____

_____

# THE CHOICE OF OWNERSHIP
*Action 5—Find Accountability*

Hopefully, you have found freedom in being transparent and sharing your life with someone else. As you continue this journey, the involvement and engagement with other people is very important. Dr. Mark Laaser says, "to achieve true change, a person must be accountable to others to make that change." Other people cannot make you change, but they are important to the process of change and experiencing freedom in your life. The key principle to this is accountability.

In your own words, what is accountability?

_____
_____
_____
_____
_____

The word "accountability" is often misunderstood and misapplied. In some churches or religious circles, it is used to convince people to confess or share their sins with others. And that is a part of it, but not a complete or inviting picture of accountability. By definition, accountability is the "ability to give an account". In the context of making changes or finding freedom from our past, our addictions and our struggles, this means we need to be able to account for our thoughts, feelings and behaviors.

In order to practice good accountability, you have to understand the interactive dynamic between your thoughts and feelings, and how that impacts your behavior. Everything we do—our behavior—starts with a thought and/or a feeling. So you must develop an ability to account for your own thoughts and feelings, and that will help you determine and change your behavior.

But, the difficulty is taking the time to reflect and identify your thoughts and feelings. You often operate on cruise control, where you don't actively consider the reactive, automatic thoughts or feelings, and then allow them to dictate your behavior. When you can identify and become accountable for your thoughts and feelings, you can start to change your behavior, which leads to the change and freedom you are seeking. This process is key to experiencing freedom in your life.

How often to do you stop and consider your thoughts and feelings? What does that look like in your life?

_____

_____

_____

_____

_____

What are some of the feelings or thoughts that typically accompany your addiction, struggle or destructive habit in your life?

_____

_____

_____

_____

_____

What fears or hesitations do you have about finding this type of accountability in your life, and sharing your thoughts, feelings and behavior?

_____

_____

_____

_____

_____

Often, people think about accountability as confrontational, where a person like your boss is making sure you do your job. And in this mindset, if you mess up, or miss the mark, then you will be in trouble when that person. But that is not an accurate description of Christian accountability. Instead, you can develop accountability with the people you trust and know that they have your best interest, and they are there to help not hurt you. They are not going to shame you, or discourage you, but rather partner with you to help keep to the commitments and growth you desire for your life change.

There are several scriptures that help guide us into good accountability and help us develop a heart and understanding for accountability.

> *"Therefore confess your sins to each other and pray for each other so that*
> *you may be healed. The prayer of a righteous person is powerful and effective."*
> —James 5:16 (NIV)

This would indicate that you are responsible to report out, or to confess, or to share our thoughts, feelings and behavior to another believer. This can be a powerful truth that will help you see the darkness in your life, and bring it into the light. And the other person can help you by praying, and in doing so, help you overcome the obstacles you have in your thinking, feeling or behavior.

> *"As iron sharpens iron, so one person sharpens another."*
> —Proverbs 27:17

This scripture describes how the process of accountability is mutually beneficial. This means that we all can be sharpened or it will benefit or help both you and the other person, when we have accountability. As much as you may need to be accountable, it is important that you can help the other person and give them accountability too.

> *"And let us consider how we may spur one another on toward love and good deeds"*
> —Hebrews 10:24

Through this accountability, the goal is to spur each other on to love and good deeds. This means that the conversations and confessions should be given and received in a tone of love and encouragement. The feedback given should help each other grow in our walk with Christ, and also towards our life change.

Finding good accountability in your life can be such a blessing and positive experience. A good accountability partner is someone who cares about you and would be willing to walk with you in a open, honest and transparent way. They can relate to you, either with similar struggles or other struggles, and understand the importance and mutual benefit of accountability in their own life. They may or may not be in a recovery process, but they should share a belief in God, and commit to praying for you and asking you the hard questions. They need to be available to you in a consistent manner, whether by phone call or face-to-face meetings, so that you can stay accountable on a regular basis. You want to find someone who can help you process your feelings and emotions, can listen to you well and provide good, solid wisdom as feedback.

This may seem like a tall order, but it is important that you find and identify these people in your life. Hopefully, some of the members of your Freedom Group can fill this role. Possibly other members at your church or Bible study can help too. Just take a minute to give them a call and ask them, "will you be my accountability partner?"

It is recommended that you have more than one or two accountability partners, so that you can have several people to call in case of crisis or trouble. Yet, the key point to accountability is having somebody. Making these life changes requires help from others, and accountability is important to the process.

Who are possible people you can trust, to partner with you and give you accountability?

1. _____

2. _____

3. _____

# THE CHOICE TO HEAL

*Action 1—Understand Forgiveness*

After looking at the complete picture of your life, including all your hurts, traumas and destructive patterns, the next choice is to heal it. Actually, the healing is not something you can do on your own, but something that God will do in you as you take certain actions that join Him in the healing process. Believe it or not, the biggest part of the healing process is forgiveness.

What is your understanding of forgiveness?

_____

_____

_____

_____

_____

Forgiveness is often a very difficult process to understand and apply. Your experiences with forgiveness, whether positive or negative, have shaped your view of forgiveness in your own life.

Can you identify with any of these thoughts on forgiveness? (circle the ones you identify with)

- Forgiveness is forgetting
- Forgiveness is reconciling
- Forgiveness is condoning
- Forgiveness is a feeling
- Forgiveness is about the person who hurt you

What experiences have led you to any of the above thoughts on forgiveness?

_____

_____

_____

_____

_____

Let's look at each of those misconceptions:

- **"Forgiveness is forgetting"**—This is not a completely accurate understanding of forgiveness. Forgiveness is not forgetting what happened or being void of the emotion of being hurt or wounded. Forgiveness is the commitment to view it from God's perspective, not our human viewpoint, and to make the choice to not let the offense hold power over you.
- **"Forgiveness is reconciling"**—Forgiveness does not automatically make everything right again. Reconciliation and forgiveness are two separate processes. You CAN forgive without reconciling, but you CAN'T reconcile without forgiveness.
- **"Forgiveness is condoning"**—When you forgive someone, it doesn't mean what they did was right. It means they don't owe anything for the pain or hurt they caused.
- **"Forgiveness is a feeling"**—Forgiveness is a choice, not feeling—because if we waited until we "felt" like forgiving—we would never forgive. God's forgiveness is a promise He makes, not conditional on any feeling, but rather the truth of the choice He makes to forgive.
- **"Forgiveness is about the person who hurt you"**—In reality, true forgiveness is more about you than it is the other person. When you choose not to forgive, it allows a root of bitterness and sin in your life that will only continue to hurt you, not them.

So, what is true forgiveness? At the most basic level, ***forgiveness is the decision to pardon an offense and give up the right to be repaid.*** When we are seeking freedom, this means that forgiveness is a gift given to us by God, through the sacrifice of His son Jesus. The result is that Jesus' death on the cross pays for the offense of our sins so that we can be forgiven.

> *"But God showed his great love for us by sending*
> *Christ to die for us while we were still sinners."*
> —Romans 5:8 (NLT)

Jesus Christ died for your sins and paid for your forgiveness. Forgiveness isn't something that we can earn, it's something that we receive. It is not a direct action we take, but a decision we make. It is something that we choose to give or receive.

After hearing what forgiveness is, what do you think forgiveness looks like and feels like in your life?

_____

_____

_____

_____

_____

What is holding you back from experiencing forgiveness?

_____

_____

_____

_____

You may struggle with forgiveness because of the shame and guilt attached to the actions that need forgiving. The memory of your actions, or the feelings you have experienced from them, can hold you back from experiencing the freedom and healing of forgiveness. In these moments, you can hold onto God's truth in Psalm 103:12, ***"He has removed our sins as far from us as the east is from the west."*** This scripture brings promise, comfort and hope that when you ask for forgiveness, God completely removes your sin, and remembers it no more. He removes the shame and guilt and replaces them with His truth.

What does Psalm 103:12, mean to you personally?

_____

_____

_____

_____

_____

Forgiveness doesn't mean that there will be no consequences for our actions. We can rest assured that the penalty for our actions has been paid by Christ and we are free to move forward and walk in responsibility.

What possible consequences might you still experience because of your sin?

_____

_____

_____

_____

_____

When we ask for forgiveness our part is turning away from what we have done. This means that we cannot keep doing the same thing over and over again. Because we are forgiven, our heart response should be to turn away and change our behavior. Paul challenges us in Romans 6:1-2a, *"What shall we say, then? Shall we go on sinning so that grace may increase? By no means!"*

The key to healing your life is to understand, accept, and apply the principle of forgiveness to your life. As you work through the next few lessons, you will be challenged to practically apply forgiveness in several areas of your life. This will help propel you forward in your healing and freedom!

# THE CHOICE TO HEAL

*Action 2—Receive Forgiveness*

Often, one of the hardest aspects of forgiveness is the ability to receive and experience forgiveness. Many people tend to get stuck in thinking that their sin or offense, is worse than everyone else's. This can bring extra remorse, shame or guilt, which paralyzes you with thoughts like, "can I ***really*** be forgiven?"

Have you ever struggled with feeling like your sin or offense was greater, or too great to be forgiven? What were your thoughts or excuses about your sinful actions?

_____

_____

_____

_____

_____

To fully understand forgiveness, you have to recognize that our sin is viewed the same in God's eyes. No one person's sin, offense or struggle is any greater than another person's. We are all equal when it comes to needing forgiveness from our past actions. Romans 3:23 tells us, ***"For everyone has sinned; we all fall short of God's glorious standard."***

How does it make you feel to know that all sins are equal in God's eyes? Is this helpful for you?

_____

_____

_____

_____

_____

Sometimes, you may allow your human experience to frame your interaction with God. When you think about how people have hurt you, or how you have hurt others, you may allow your pain or shame to block your connection to God. But in your relationship with God, there is no pain or shame, but love, mercy, and total forgiveness. Forgiveness is important because it gives you a pathway to move forward breaking you free from the hurts of your past.

Have you ever experienced forgiveness with another person? How did that shape your perspective on forgiveness?

_____

_____

_____

_____

_____

The mercy and forgiveness from God is unlike any human experience. God's forgiveness gives you freedom and restores your relationship with Him and others, in a way you could not attain on your own. No amount of works or deeds can be done to earn or justify God's forgiveness.

In fact, forgiveness is not something that you can earn or that you even deserve. Jesus died on the cross so that you could be forgiven. Knowing this is important because many people think that God could never forgive them without some payment or work in return. Instead, God paid that price for you. He sacrificed His son, Jesus, as the payment for your sins.

In your life, has anyone sacrificed anything for you? How did that make you feel?

_____

_____

_____

_____

_____

In Paul's letter to Titus, he writes the following verses, ***"⁴ But—When God our Savior revealed his kindness and love, ⁵ he saved us, not because of the righteous things we had done, but because of his mercy. He washed away our sins, giving us a new birth and new life through the Holy Spirit. ⁶ He generously poured out the Spirit upon us through Jesus Christ our Savior.⁷ Because of his grace he made us right in his sight and gave us confidence that we will inherit eternal life."*** —Titus 3:4-7 (NLT)

As you read that scripture, what does it say to you about the nature of God's mercy and forgiveness?

_____

_____

_____

_____

_____

Another important thing to remember is that forgiveness is a gift we can either receive or reject. You have the choice to make. God is always willing to forgive. It's not that God won't forgive you, it's that you choose what to do with His forgiveness. If you say that you don't want God's forgiveness, you are keeping yourself in a prison. Statements or thoughts that God could never forgive what you have done are basically saying Jesus Christ's death wasn't enough for you.

When considering God's forgiveness of our sins, we must look at the process. Remember, forgiveness is not something we earn, but we do play a part. 1 John 1:9 promises, ***"If we confess our sins, he is faithful and just and will forgive us our sins and purify us from all unrighteousness."*** (NIV) This action requires humbling ourselves and confessing to God thoughts, words, or actions that we need forgiveness for.

What do you need to confess to God that you need forgiveness for?

_____

_____

_____

_____

_____

_____

_____

Often, you may feel that God could not forgive what you have done, which results in you feeling like you can't forgive yourself. But, when you say that you could never forgive yourself, you are holding yourself to a higher standard than God does. Instead, you can experience freedom through confession and repentance. Repenting means that you actively turn away from what you have done and confessed. You must demonstrate a desire to change, not continue living with your destructive habits, addictions or struggles. The goal would be to stop the destructive behavior and start living in the freedom and healing God provides through forgiveness.

Repentance means turning away from your sin. What would this look like in your life? What actions do you need to take in order to turn away from your destructive behaviors or struggles?

_____

_____

_____

_____

_____

Once you have confessed and repented, you only need to ask for forgiveness. This is where you can humbly and simply ask God to forgive what you have done. It is not a fancy, theological statement, but rather a heart-felt and honest request for forgiveness. This is simply your part of the process. God has promised to forgive us, pardon our offenses and give up the right to be repaid. He has paid the price of your sin with the death of Jesus. And He will remember your sin no more!

Write a simple prayer, asking God to forgive you for what you have done:

_____

_____

_____

_____

_____

The last part of the process is the easiest and hardest, at the same time! It is simply to accept God's forgiveness, releasing yourself from any self-condemnation, shame, guilt, or remorse you may have. Romans 8:1 makes the following declaration, *"there is no condemnation for those who are in Christ Jesus."* (NIV) This means that you can accept God's forgiveness and live free from any condemnation for your sins. There may still be consequences, but the payment of your sins has been paid, and you can accept true forgiveness from God.

This process is not a one-time event; rather a daily, moment to moment, lifelong experience. You can develop and practice confessing, repenting, asking for forgiveness, then accepting and moving forward. This will lead to the healing and freedom you seek for the struggles and destructive behavior that has held you back.

# THE CHOICE TO HEAL

*Action 3—Forgive Those Who Have Hurt Me*

It is one thing to consider that God, the Creator of heaven and earth, can forgive you. But it is an entirely different concept to forgive those who have deeply hurt or offended you. This is where forgiveness on our part is the most difficult. How does someone forgive the person who murdered his or her child? Or forgive the person who cheated on you? Or forgive the person who abused you, lied to you, betrayed you, gossiped about you or offended you in any way? Sometimes these hurts came from those we love the most or care about deeply.

Hurts and pains in life are a common human experience that everyone must learn to deal with in healthy ways. If you don't learn to handle the pain, then it will move you towards something that may hurt you or others even more. This is where forgiveness for others can bring you healing.

In your past, what hurt and pain from others have you not forgiven and held onto?

_____

_____

_____

_____

_____

Have you experienced damage in your relationships from a lack of forgiveness? What has been the result of your unforgiveness?

_____

_____

_____

_____

_____

It is important to know that forgiveness is more about you than the other person. When you choose to forgive others, you are set free and no longer controlled by them. The hurt they caused can be healed and bring you freedom from the resentment and bitterness that holds you back and keeps you enslaved to negative thought patterns. In this way, forgiveness for others is really more about you than them.

Unforgiveness leads to resentment and bitterness. How have these two feelings affected your life in the past?

_____

_____

_____

_____

_____

*"Make allowance for each other's faults, and forgive anyone who offends you. Remember, the Lord forgave you, so you must forgive others."*
– Colossians 3:13 (NLT)

God instructs you to forgive others, not so that they will get off the hook, or escape the consequences of their actions. Forgiving those who have hurt you helps to give that hurt over to God. He really wants you to be free from the resentment, bitterness, anger and pain. So forgiving others helps you to heal and experience freedom.

Read the following scriptures and identify how they apply to forgiveness:

*"Get rid of all bitterness, rage, anger, harsh words, and slander, as well as all types of evil behavior. <sup>32</sup> Instead, be kind to each other, tenderhearted, forgiving one another, just as God through Christ has forgiven you."*
—Ephesians 4:31-32 (NLT)

_____

_____

_____

_____

_____

*"Never pay back evil with more evil. Do things in such a way that everyone can see you are honorable. <sup>18</sup> Do all that you can to live in peace with everyone."*
—Romans 12:17-19 (NLT)

_____

_____

_____

_____

_____

The process of forgiving others is simple enough in practical steps but requires a trust in God for the outcome. In the next few pages, you will walk through these steps for forgiveness.

If you need more space or have more people to forgive, then use this same format on a separate sheet of paper. This is an activity you may do several different times, and hopefully becomes a useful tool in your life.

**Steps to Forgiveness**
1. Identify the person who has hurt you.
2. Name what they done to you (lied, cheated, abused, etc.).
3. Figure out what they owe you (an apology, the truth or an explanation).
4. Give up your right to hurt them or get even.
5. Give them over to God and forgive them.

| Who Hurt You? | What did they do to you? | What do they owe you? | Are you ready to give them over to God? |
|---|---|---|---|
|  |  |  | YES<br>NO |
|  |  |  | YES<br>NO |
|  |  |  | YES<br>NO |
|  |  |  | YES<br>NO |
|  |  |  | YES<br>NO |
|  |  |  | YES<br>NO |
|  |  |  | YES<br>NO |
|  |  |  | YES<br>NO |

Next, if you are ready to give them over to God and give up the right to get even or hurt them, then you will now write their names below and spend time praying through each name and situation. Let God know that you are giving the person and the offense over to Him and that you trust that He will heal your hurt and help you move forward in freedom. This may take more than one prayer and may take several times sitting down and going through this exercise. Be sure to take your time and really be authentic and honest in your heart about your intentions to forgive each person. If this is difficult, then ask for help from your group leader or someone who has done this.

| Name of Person to Forgive | Date I prayed to forgive: |
| --- | --- |
|  |  |
|  |  |
|  |  |
|  |  |
|  |  |
|  |  |
|  |  |
|  |  |
|  |  |
|  |  |
|  |  |
|  |  |
|  |  |

After completing this exercise, you may wonder if you really forgave them. How will you know? Here's how: as you continue through life, you will be free to think about or interact with them, without bitterness, resentment or feelings of anger. You won't avoid them or say hurtful things them. You will continue to pray for them, and not think about getting even with them.

Reflect on your experience forgiving others, and journal how it feels to give them to God, not allowing their offense or actions to hurt you anymore and have control over you.

_____

_____

_____

_____

_____

_____

_____

_____

_____

_____

_____

_____

_____

_____

_____

_____

_____

_____

_____

_____

_____

# THE CHOICE TO HEAL

*Action 4—Ask Forgiveness from Those I Have Hurt Part 1*

After receiving forgiveness from God, and working through forgiving others, it is time to consider the other side of forgiveness. This is your chance to acknowledge that you have hurt others, own the damage you have created, and be willing to ask for forgiveness. This is the process of healing and restoring relationships that you have hurt by your struggles or destructive behavior.

This is an opportunity to overcome guilt, shame, and self-condemnation, and do whatever is necessary to mend bridges with those you have hurt. You will need to humble yourself and ask for forgiveness for your actions, without regard to the other person's response.

> *"So if you are presenting a sacrifice at the altar in the Temple and you suddenly remember that someone has something against you, leave your sacrifice there at the altar. Go and be reconciled to that person. Then come and offer your sacrifice to God."*
> —Matthew 5:23-24 (NLT)

Jesus spoke these words to you, to help you understand how urgent your responsibility is to take action towards reconciliation and restoration of damaged relationships. You must own what you have done to hurt the relationship, and then do everything that you can to restore it. This doesn't mean that the other person will forgive you; that is their decision. Your part is humbling yourself, asking for forgiveness, and be willing to take steps to make right, what was damaged or hurt.

There is a process of coming to terms with what you have done. And there is also the challenge of taking responsibility for your actions and the pain caused by them. What may be some roadblocks to this process?

_____
_____
_____
_____
_____
_____
_____

Our responsibility is to own what we have done. Everything within us says, don't do it! It is natural human tendency to come up with excuses like:

- It happened so long ago.
- They don't even live around here anymore.
- What good will it do anyway?
- They won't understand.
- I will do it later.

Remember, making excuses will prevent you from moving forward. We need to do what God tells us to do because we will benefit from doing the right thing.

What are some of the reasons you have not made amends by asking for forgiveness? Or what excuses have you used to ignore these behaviors or situations?

_____
_____
_____
_____
_____
_____
_____

Prayerfully think back to the damage and harm you have caused in your relationships. How have you harmed others? What types of things do you need to ask forgiveness for?

_____

_____

_____

_____

_____

_____

_____

_____

Take a moment to pray asking God for help with this next task of making a list. Think about the people and relationships you have hurt, and what exact harm was done to the relationship by your actions. If necessary, use another sheet of paper to continue the list.

| Person I harmed: | Relationship: | I caused harm when and the effect was: |
|---|---|---|
|  |  |  |
|  |  |  |
|  |  |  |
|  |  |  |
|  |  |  |
|  |  |  |

| Person I harmed: | Relationship: | I caused harm when and the effect was: |
|---|---|---|
| | | |
| | | |
| | | |
| | | |
| | | |

Obviously, it may not be possible to make a direct amend or ask forgiveness from every person on your list. A ***direct amend*** should be made to those who are readily accessible and who can be approached when you are ready. An ***indirect amend*** can be made in situations that may prevent us from making a direct personal contact. Here are some options and guidelines for making direct and indirect amends:

    a.  **Face to Face**—This is the most direct, and usually the best, method to make an amend in the relationship. If possible, set up a time to talk to the person face to face and discuss what you have done that caused them harm.

    b.  **Phone Call**—If the person lives far away or meeting them face to face would not be safe or wise, then making a phone call would be a good option. You can still call and discuss what you have done that caused them harm.

    c.  **Letter**—You can also write a letter to someone who does not have a phone or cannot be reached in another way, for whatever possible reason. This would be a less direct amend but can still work as a way to take responsibility for your actions. Be sure not to allow this option to keep you from making face to face or phone call, but only when the person is difficult to reach.

    d.  **Symbolic**—This would be the least direct way of making amend. It can be used for someone you don't know or cannot contact. In this amend process, you will write a letter to the person explaining what you have done to them, ask forgiveness, then read it out loud to an empty chair.

There may be people you may not be able to make amends or restitution to, because complete disclosure could cause harm to them or others. This does not provide a loophole or an escape clause for you not to make amends. Instead, this should motivate us to analyze and consider the circumstances and specific situations that could result in more damage being done. This could include employers, ex-partners, former business associates, spouses, or friends. Please be very careful to examine your heart and seek wise counsel before making exceptions to your list.

As you come up with a plan for making an amend and asking for forgiveness, remember not to justify why you did or said it. Just take responsibility for your actions and "clean your side of the street".

Complete the following action plan for each amend that you need to make. Write out the details of what you are making the amend for, what type of restitution or reconciliation you can offer, and identify anything you may need help with. Be sure to determine if the amend should be face to face, phone call, letter or symbolic. Write out the date you completed each amend. If necessary, use another sheet of paper to continue the plan.

Name of Person: _____

Circle Method:    *face to face    phone call    letter    symbolic*

| For what should I make amends? | What restitution or offer of reconciliation should I prepare for? | Is there anything I need to discuss with mentor or support person? | **Date Amend Completed** |
|---|---|---|---|
|  |  |  |  |

Name of Person: _____

Circle Method:    *face to face   phone call    letter   symbolic*

| For what should I make amends? | What restitution or offer of reconciliation should I prepare for? | Is there anything I need to discuss with mentor or support person? | **Date Amend Completed** |
|---|---|---|---|
|  |  |  |  |

Name of Person: _____

Circle Method:    *face to face   phone call    letter   symbolic*

| For what should I make amends? | What restitution or offer of reconciliation should I prepare for? | Is there anything I need to discuss with mentor or support person? | **Date Amend Completed** |
|---|---|---|---|
|  |  |  |  |

Name of Person: _____

Circle Method:  *face to face   phone call   letter   symbolic*

| For what should I make amends? | What restitution or offer of reconciliation should I prepare for? | Is there anything I need to discuss with mentor or support person? | **Date Amend Completed** |
|---|---|---|---|
| | | | |

Name of Person: _____

Circle Method:  *face to face   phone call   letter   symbolic*

| For what should I make amends? | What restitution or offer of reconciliation should I prepare for? | Is there anything I need to discuss with mentor or support person? | **Date Amend Completed** |
|---|---|---|---|
| | | | |

Name of Person: _____

Circle Method:  *face to face   phone call   letter   symbolic*

| For what should I make amends? | What restitution or offer of reconciliation should I prepare for? | Is there anything I need to discuss with mentor or support person? | **Date Amend Completed** |
|---|---|---|---|
|  |  |  |  |

Name of Person: _____

Circle Method:  *face to face   phone call   letter   symbolic*

| For what should I make amends? | What restitution or offer of reconciliation should I prepare for? | Is there anything I need to discuss with mentor or support person? | **Date Amend Completed** |
|---|---|---|---|
|  |  |  |  |

Name of Person: _____

Circle Method:   *face to face   phone call   letter   symbolic*

| For what should I make amends? | What restitution or offer of reconciliation should I prepare for? | Is there anything I need to discuss with mentor or support person? | **Date Amend Completed** |
|---|---|---|---|
|  |  |  |  |

Name of Person: _____

Circle Method:   *face to face   phone call   letter   symbolic*

| For what should I make amends? | What restitution or offer of reconciliation should I prepare for? | Is there anything I need to discuss with mentor or support person? | **Date Amend Completed** |
|---|---|---|---|
|  |  |  |  |

# THE CHOICE TO HEAL

*Action 4—Ask Forgiveness from Those I Have Hurt Part 2*

When you make the choice to heal and embrace the process of forgiveness, you take action towards a life of freedom! You can be free from the shame and guilt from your past with God's forgiveness. You can live free of resentment and bitterness when you choose to forgive others. Most of all, you are free from the chains of brokenness and hurt relationships when you seek forgiveness from those you have hurt.

As you seek forgiveness by making amends, you will learn that this process doesn't come easy and takes time. It is rare that you will recognize your offenses and make amends in a short time span of a week. It usually takes longer because you will encounter many emotions and obstacles. You should have people in your life that can help and support you this process.

List some supportive people in your life that may have helped, or could help you take this next step in your journey to freedom?

1. _____
2. _____
3. _____

Often, the support you can receive from others will help as you work to muster the courage and resolution to take the hard difficult action of asking for forgiveness. This is where other members of your freedom group and your group leader can be of great benefit!

What were some of your feelings you had before, during and after your making amends?

Before, I felt ————————————————————————————————

During, I felt ————————————————————————————————

After, I felt ————————————————————————————————

God's word can also be an encouragement and give great direction for you as you engage in this life-long skill of asking for forgiveness. Read the following scriptures and write down the encouragement and direction given by God:

**Philippians 2:3-4** "³ *Do nothing out of selfish ambition or vain conceit. Rather, in humility value others above yourselves,* ⁴ *not looking to your own interests but each of you to the interests of the others.*" (NIV)

————————————————————————————————————

————————————————————————————————————

————————————————————————————————————

————————————————————————————————————

————————————————————————————————————

**1 Peter 4:8-10** "⁸ *Above all, love each other deeply, because love covers over a multitude of sins.*⁹ *Offer hospitality to one another without grumbling.* ¹⁰ *Each of you should use whatever gift you have received to serve others, as faithful stewards of God's grace in its various forms.*" (NIV)

————————————————————————————————————

————————————————————————————————————

————————————————————————————————————

————————————————————————————————————

**Psalms 51:14-17** "¹⁴*Forgive me for shedding blood, O God who saves; then I will joyfully sing of your forgiveness.* ¹⁵*Unseal my lips, O Lord, that my mouth may praise you.*¹⁶ *You do not desire a sacrifice, or I would offer one. You do not want a burnt offering.*¹⁷ *The sacrifice you desire is a broken spirit. You will not reject a broken and repentant heart, O God.*" (NLT)

————————————————————————————————————

————————————————————————————————————

————————————————————————————————————

————————————————————————————————————

**Romans 14:13** "¹³ *Therefore let us stop passing judgment on one another. Instead, make up your mind not to put any stumbling block or obstacle in the way of a brother or sister.*" (NIV)

_____

_____

_____

_____

_____

_____

By now, you have already taken the time and initiative to make your amends and ask for forgiveness. What were some of your experiences and favorite conversations?

_____

_____

_____

_____

_____

_____

_____

_____

_____

_____

_____

What is something about this process that surprised you?

_____

_____

_____

_____

_____

_____

_____

_____

_____

What did you learn about yourself or others during this process?

_____

_____

_____

_____

_____

_____

_____

What did you learn about Jesus and your relationship with God during this process of making amends?

_____

_____

_____

_____

_____

_____

_____

_____

_____

_____

_____

How do you feel about these relationships after you made your amends?

_____

_____

_____

_____

_____

_____

_____

_____

_____

_____

Making amends will be a life-long process; you will need to ask for forgiveness again in the future. What have you learned from this experience that will help you in the future?

_____

_____

_____

_____

_____

_____

_____

_____

_____

_____

_____

_____

# THE CHOICE TO GROW

## Action 1—Change our Thinking

As we walk through the choice to **Grow**, our goal is to experience true freedom. It is not enough to change our behavior like anger, overeating, drugs or alcohol without looking at those things that drive the behavior. One of the most important areas to look at and change is our belief.

What we believe will have a direct effect on our behaviors. Think about it this way; what we believe affects how we think, how we think affects what we do and what we do leads to the outcomes in our lives. In 2 Corinthians 10:5 it says, ***We demolish arguments and every pretension that sets itself up against the knowledge of God, and we take captive every thought to make it obedient to Christ.*** The battle of thoughts happens by distorting our view of God and our view of ourselves. If we do not have correct thinking and beliefs about these two areas, then it will be difficult if not impossible to experience freedom.

If you were to describe God, how would you describe Him? (Use as many descriptive words as you can)

_____

_____

_____

_____

_____

Read each of the verses below and write the different qualities of God.

**Exodus 34:6-7** *"Yahweh! The Lord! The God of compassion and mercy! I am slow to anger and filled with unfailing love and faithfulness. I lavish unfailing love to a thousand generations. I forgive iniquity, rebellion, and sin."*

_____

_____

_____

_____

_____

**Jeremiah 10:12** *"But the Lord made the earth by his power, and he preserves it by his wisdom. With his own understanding he stretched out the heavens."*

_____

_____

_____

_____

_____

**Micah 7:18-19** *"Where is another God like you, who pardons the guilt of the remnant, overlooking the sins of his special people? You will not stay angry with your people forever, because you delight in showing unfailing love. Once again you will have compassion on us. You will trample our sins under your feet and throw them into the depths of the ocean!"*

_____

_____

_____

_____

_____

How has the description in the Bible line up with the description that you wrote earlier? And what differences did you discover?

_____

_____

_____

_____

The other battle is in the thinking about ourselves. The bible says that when we become a Christ follower than we become a new person. But depending on what we have experienced throughout our lifetime, there are sure to be false beliefs. These beliefs can make us feel insecure and devalued. This can happen through our failures and by the things that people have said about us and done to us.

If you were to describe yourself to someone in two short sentences, what would you say?

_____

_____

_____

_____

_____

Look at the following verses and write down how God sees us.

**1 Peter 2:9** *"But you are not like that, for you are a chosen people. You are royal priests, a holy nation, God's very own possession. As a result, you can show others the goodness of God, for he called you out of the darkness into his wonderful light."*

_____

_____

_____

_____

_____

**Ephesians 2:10** *"For we are God's masterpiece. He has created us anew in Christ Jesus, so we can do the good things he planned for us long ago."*

_____

_____

_____

_____

_____

The way that we change our false beliefs is by first identifying them and secondly by replacing them with God's truth. It can be difficult to identify these beliefs, but as you read the list below, I want you to ask yourself how true each statement sounds to you. If you identify with it or if you know that you believe it, then place a check beside each one.

☐    I must please other people in order to be loved or accepted

☐    I am unworthy of love and acceptance

☐    I must have respect to know I have value

☐    I must perform or achieve to be accepted

☐    What I do makes me who I am

☐    Other people must meet my needs

☐    I do not measure up

☐    I am a failure

☐    I'm worthless

☐    In order to feel worthy, I must not fail

☐    Others cannot be trusted

☐    I must take care of myself

☐    I do not need to change or I will never change

☐    If I'm vulnerable I will get hurt

☐    I must earn love

☐    I don't need anyone

☐    My value is in my appearance

☐    Asking for help is a sign of weakness

Write each false belief and the effect that it has on you and your view of God

| False Belief | Effect on me and view of God |
|---|---|
| *Example:*<br>*I must please other people to be loved or accepted* | *Example:*<br>*I am always appeasing others, or adjusting for them, not true to myself. I view God as one them I am trying to please, and can never measure up.* |
|  |  |
|  |  |

| False Belief | Effect on me and view of God |
|---|---|
| | |
| | |
| | |
| | |

*(If you need more space, use back of the page or extra sheet of paper)*

Look at each false belief that you checked and match it with the statements of truth below.

- ☐ I am to please God rather than seek the approval of people
- ☐ Nothing can separate you from the love of God
- ☐ True respect and honor comes from God, not people
- ☐ God accepts me just as I am not because of what I do
- ☐ What I do does not define who I am
- ☐ God is the only one that can meet my needs
- ☐ Through Christ, I am enough
- ☐ God is proud of who I am
- ☐ I am valuable and loved in God's eyes
- ☐ God loves me for who I am not what I do
- ☐ God is trustworthy
- ☐ God will meet all of your needs
- ☐ Through Christ all thing become new
- ☐ My strength is in Christ

- ☐ God gave His life because He loves me
- ☐ I need Christ and others to help me grow
- ☐ My value is in Christ
- ☐ I can do all things through Christ who gives me strength

How does it make you feel when you read the false belief and then the truth?

_____

_____

_____

_____

_____

_____

_____

_____

_____

_____

_____

_____

_____

# THE CHOICE TO GROW
## Action 2—Embrace Our Identity

As you continue your journey, you will need to reflect on and determine what you believe. And this will not only involve your belief system and way of thinking, but also what you believe about your identity, or who you really are. In order to experience true freedom, you have to really embrace and understanding your identity.

We all want to know who we are. We seek and search, and we try to "find ourselves." Too often, we base our identity and self-worth on things of this world and the culture around us. You may base your identity on your looks, your job or career, how much money and possessions you have, or your education or accomplishments. You may gain your understanding of yourself from what others have told you or what you've been taught growing up. This leads to building our reputation, but not the truth of our identity. Your reputation has probably been shaped by your past experiences or behavior, your success or failures, or even your relationships. But when you build your identity and self-concept on these worldly and cultural influences, they usually lead to dissatisfaction and disappointment.

Your identity affects everything about you. It impacts the way you think, the way you feel, what you do, and who you are becoming. And when we seek our identity in the wrong places and things, then we place our life on shaky ground. There has to be a more solid foundation to build our identity. When the pressure of life comes, the things of this world will crumble and fail you. But when you seek and embrace your true identity, then you can begin to grow and flourish.

If you were to describe who you are, what would you say?

_____

_____

_____

_____

_____

What is your earliest memory of when you came to understand your identity apart from your parents or family?

_____

_____

_____

_____

_____

What people or influences in your life have shaped your concept of who you are? How did that impact your life, negative or positive?

_____

_____

_____

_____

_____

What are some of the worldly or cultural values you have placed your identity in?

_____

_____

_____

_____

_____

When you understand where you have placed your identity, then you can better understand how you may have developed struggles or addictions. Often, your biggest obstacles in life have come from a place of insecurity or fear, based out of a misconception of who you are.

Do you believe that you can view yourself differently? If not, why?

_____

_____

_____

_____

_____

Growth can occur when you begin to change your view of yourself and embrace your identity in Jesus Christ. This identity is based out of your growing relationship with Him, and learning "who" God says you are through His word, the Bible. Since God created you and knows you inside and out, it only makes sense to turn to Him to find your true identity.

1 Corinthians 5:17 says this, *"Therefore, if anyone is in Christ, he is a new creation; the old has passed away, and see, the new has come!" This is a bold declaration of who you become when you are in relationship with Jesus."*

What does it mean to you to be considered a new creation?

_____

_____

_____

_____

_____

Since you are a new creation and have a relationship with Jesus Christ, then God's word has a lot to say about your identity. Look at the following scriptures and write down what God says about you:

*1 John 3:1* *"See what great love the Father has given us that we should be called God's children—and we are! The reason the world does not know us is that it didn't know him."*

_____

_____

_____

_____

_____

*1 Peter 2:24* "He himself bore our sins in his body on the tree; so that, having died to sins, we might live for righteousness. By his wounds you have been healed."

_____

_____

_____

_____

_____

_____

*Ephesians 1:4-5* "For he chose us in him, before the foundation of the world, to be holy and blameless in love before him. He predestined us to be adopted as sons through Jesus Christ for himself, according to the good pleasure of his will"

_____

_____

_____

_____

_____

_____

*Deuteronomy 31:8* "The Lord is the one who will go before you. He will be with you; he will not leave you or abandon you. Do not be afraid or discouraged."

_____

_____

_____

_____

_____

*Romans 8:37* "No, in all these things we are more than conquerors through him who loved us."

_____

_____

_____

_____

_____

***Galatians 5:1*** *"For freedom, Christ set us free. Stand firm then and don't submit again to a yoke of slavery."*

_____

_____

_____

_____

_____

***Ephesians 2:8*** *"For you are saved by grace through faith, and this is not from yourselves; it is God's gift"*

_____

_____

_____

_____

_____

Now that you have learned what God says about you, and how He views you, you can walk in the truth of your new identity in Christ. One way to solidify this new self-concept is to practice self-affirmations. You can take these scriptures and create statements and positive realizations about your identity in Christ, and speak them every day for the next month. Take 5-10 minutes every day and read them out loud and ask God to help you bury these in your heart and shape a new identity, your true and authentic identity in Jesus Christ!

# THE CHOICE TO GROW

*Action 3—Identify and Replace*

As you continue to grow, you must understand how your old identity and core beliefs have impacted your life. They have created characteristics or patterns of thought and behavior that we can start to categorize as defects of character.

A defect of your character could be described as a flaw, a weakness or a shortcoming. Which just means that we aren't perfect. Part of your growth process will be identifying these defects and replacing them. Just like you would cut out the diseased and unhealthy branches of a plant or tree, so that the plant can be healthy. You have the choice to cut out the unhealthy characteristics of your life, and let God help you create new ones to replace them.

Ephesians 4:21-24 explains the process of putting off the characteristics of your past and replacing them with Godly characteristics: ***"if indeed you have heard Him and have been taught by Him, as the truth is in Jesus: that you put off, concerning your former conduct, the old man which grows corrupt according to the deceitful lusts, and be renewed in the spirit of your mind, and that you put on the new man which was created according to God, in true righteousness and holiness."***

Look at this list and circle the character defects you need to "put off". The list is not all-inclusive, so you can also add other characteristics you feel need to be replaced. (fill in blanks at bottom in necessary)

| | | | |
|---|---|---|---|
| Anger | Dishonesty | Laziness | Critical Spirit |
| Bitterness | Dependency | Perfectionism | Disrespect |
| Harsh Words | Fear | Judging | Disobedience |
| Arrogance | Gluttony | Resentment | Hatred |
| Selfishness | Greed | Rebellion | Irresponsibility |
| Stubbornness | Gossiping | Argumentative | Pride |
| Controlling | Impatience | Infidelity | Lust |
| Manipulating | Intolerance | Cheating | Self Pity |
| Lying | Jealousy | Complaining | Undisciplined |

_____

_____

_____

_____

_____

If you have a hard time identifying or recognizing negative characteristics in your life, then take some time to ask someone you who knows you well and you trust their feedback and input in your life. Often, we are blinded from our worst characteristics, but those closest to us have been affected by them and can recognize them more easily.

Who is the person(s) closest to you that you trust can help you in this process?

_____

_____

_____

_____

Ephesians 4:31 says *"Get rid of all bitterness, rage, anger, harsh words, and slander, as well as all types of evil behavior."*

What are some steps you can take to "get rid of" or "put off" these negative characteristics?

_____

_____

_____

_____

_____

There are always reasons why we have developed these character traits in our life. Some of these characteristics have served you well, and may have helped you cope with traumas or experiences of life. Some characteristics will be hard to release because they have been our automatic mode of operation for so long. But, if the character trait is a negative pattern in your life, then it will only hinder your growth.

How have these characteristics helped you or protected you in your life?

_____

_____

_____

_____

_____

Now that you are in this process of life change and growth, these characteristics are not helpful. In fact, to continue in these patterns of behavior will only negatively impact your growth process and can actually lead you back to relapse or slipping back to old patterns of life. In order to eliminate these defects in your life, you will need God's help.

Next, take time to stop and pray. Ask God to help you determine how to eliminate these defects of character and what you will need to replace them with.

Prayer:

_____

_____

_____

_____

_____

The following is a list of biblical traits you can use to replace your defects of character. Take the time to pray through the list and see which of these can best replace the negative traits you circled or identified earlier. Use the chart of the following page to write down your negative character traits and the character traits you wish to replace them with.

| | | | |
|---|---|---|---|
| Love | Compassion | Knowledge | Reconciliation |
| Joy | Forgiveness | Grace | Careful words |
| Peace | Thanksgiving | Mercy | Truthful |
| Patience | Purity | Calmness | Encouragement |
| Kindness | Humility | Hope | Submission |
| Goodness | Holiness | Trust | Respect |
| Faithfulness | Honesty | Hospitality | Contentment |
| Gentleness | Wisdom | Perseverance | Discipline |
| Self-control | Discernment | Endurance | Gratefulness |

| Defect of Character | Godly Trait | Steps to Replace |
|---|---|---|
| *Example:* <br> *Dishonesty* | *Example:* <br> *Truthfulness, Honesty* | *Example:* <br> *1. Identify things I lie about—make plan to tell the truth and deal with consequences* <br> *2. Get accountable for my actions, time, thoughts—find someone to help me.* |
| | | |
| | | |
| | | |

| Defect of Character | Godly Trait | Steps to Replace |
|---|---|---|
| | | |
| | | |
| | | |
| | | |
| | | |
| | | |

| Defect of Character | Godly Trait | Steps to Replace |
|---|---|---|
| | | |
| | | |
| | | |

(If you need more space, use a separate piece of paper.)

Remember, this is a process and change won't happen overnight. You have used some of these patterns of behavior and defects for many years, and they won't go away without a struggle. And it won't happen without the help and accountability of someone who cares about you.

Determine 2-3 people you can trust to help you in this process. Tell them your list of characteristics and your possible first steps to replace them. Then, ask them to help you focus on and work on this process of identifying and replacing. These people can be very helpful to you staying focused and accountable to the changes you desire to make.

Who are the people you trust to help in this action step?

_____

_____

_____

# THE CHOICE TO GROW

*Action 4—Practice Integrity*

What does the word ***integrity*** mean to you?

_____

_____

_____

_____

_____

What does integrity have to do with your character?

_____

_____

_____

_____

_____

John Wooden, the famous Basketball coach from UCLA once said, "be more concerned with your character than your reputation, because your character is what you really are, while your reputation is merely what others think you are." You will often work hard to create a reputation among your peers or others, but this doesn't truly represent your character, or who you really are. But as you choose to grow, the next action step is to walk and live a life of character and integrity.

A person with integrity lives with honesty and strong moral principles, or moral uprightness, and is the type of person who does what they say and follows through. Integrity is all about your character, which is who you really are when no one is looking.

Who is a person of integrity in your life? What type of qualities do they possess that make them a person of integrity?

_____

_____

_____

_____

_____

In what ways have you fallen short of the goal of integrity? In what areas do you need to improve and develop integrity?

_____

_____

_____

_____

_____

Why do you think integrity is important to your life change process and experiencing freedom?

_____

_____

_____

_____

_____

The ability to live and practice integrity involves many different dynamics, but usually centers on honesty, transparency and the doing the right thing. When faced with difficulties or pressures in life, you want to become the person who can be depended on to be honest, even if being honest isn't easy. And you want to be confident in your honesty, so that you can be fully transparent and not ashamed to do what is right.

What prevents you from having integrity in difficult situations?

_____

_____

_____

_____

_____

How do you handle fear, insecurity or shame as it relates to your integrity?

_____

_____

_____

_____

_____

Integrity is often the choice between what's easy and what's right in God's eyes. It is often best demonstrated in the small, daily decisions that you make when only God is watching. In the past you may have done what feels right and justified those decisions, but in the end they didn't represent the integrity or character you would want.

How can you tell what is the right thing to do? What standard do you live by?

_____

_____

_____

_____

How can you better understand God's standard and how He wants you to live and respond with integrity?

_____

_____

_____

_____

When you start to practice integrity, you will be challenged and face difficult moments. God's word says in 1 Peter 3:13-17:

*<sup>13</sup> Who then will harm you if you are devoted to what is good? <sup>14</sup> But even if you should suffer for righteousness, you are blessed. Do not fear what they fear or be intimidated, <sup>15</sup> but in your hearts regard Christ the Lord as holy, ready at any time to give a defense to anyone who asks you for a reason for the hope that is in you. <sup>16</sup> Yet do this with gentleness and respect, keeping a clear conscience, so that when you are accused, those who disparage your good conduct in Christ will be put to shame. <sup>17</sup> For it is better to suffer for doing good, if that should be God's will, than for doing evil.*

How does this verse encourage you or give you confidence to have integrity and do what is right?

_____

_____

_____

_____

_____

_____

_____

Your lack of integrity is evident in small, daily decisions, when no one is looking. This also means that you can build, develop and practice integrity with those small, daily decisions. You can start today, and practice integrity that will help strengthen your ability to stand up under the pressure of life, and maintain your integrity and character.

In order to demonstrate your true character and integrity, you have to be willing to stand by your word, and be a man/woman who does what you say.

Matthew 5:37 says, *"Just say a simple, 'Yes, I will,' or 'No, I won't.' Anything beyond this is from the evil one."*

James 5:12 says, *"Above all, my brothers and sisters, do not swear, either by heaven or by earth or with any other oath. But let your "yes" mean "yes," and your "no" mean "no," so that you won't fall under judgment."*

Have you struggled to be a person who follows through with your word? Do you "walk the talk"?

_____

_____

_____

_____

_____

_____

_____

Today is the day to begin to practice integrity and become a person with solid character. You can become the person that others will trust to be honest, do the right thing and follow through on commitments. With God's help, you can walk with integrity and character.

# THE CHOICE TO GROW

*Action 5—Relapse Prevention*

Imagine you are riding a bike up a steep mountain road. What would happen if you stopped pedaling? Would you continue going up the mountain? Would you stay in the same spot? Or would you slip back down the mountain? Common sense and experience teaches us that we would slip back down the mountain, back to where we started.

The same dynamic and principle exists as we choose to grow and journey toward true freedom. If we choose to not continue growing or practicing the tools and principles we have learned, then we will not just stop growing, we will actually slip back to the old patterns, struggles and addictions. This is called relapse, which is when you go back to something that is harmful to you after you told yourself you wouldn't do it again.

No one wants or desires to relapse, but without paying careful attention and taking intentional action steps, it can be a very easy trap to fall into. That is why you will need to develop a habit of practicing self-awareness and honest reflection in order to keep growing and prevent relapse in your recovery journey.

What would relapse or falling back into old patterns look like for you?

_____

_____

_____

_____

There are predictable signs, indicators and patterns you will need to identify and be aware of, so that you can take the appropriate action steps to keep growing. There are four stages of slipping back into relapse, so it will be important for you to determine what your pattern is and how to avoid relapse. The stages are:

- Losing Focus
- Chaos
- Emotional Imbalance
- Burnout

Look at the following list of signs and indicators of *Losing Focus* and check off the behaviors you identify with now, or in your past:

**Losing Focus**
☐ Isolation—pull away from people who provide support and encouragement
☐ Lack of follow through on commitments and breaking promises
☐ Stop attending support or recovery groups
☐ Hiding things from others, lying or sneaky behaviors
☐ Less time or energy for God or church
☐ Avoiding accountability
☐ Surface conversations, lack of transparency or authenticity
☐ Obsession/preoccupation with hobbies, entertainment, or relationships
☐ Becoming overconfident or feeling powerful over old ways
☐ Withholding love and support from others

Of these behaviors, what are the one or two most impactful patterns for you?

_____

_____

_____

_____

_____

How do these behaviors affect you? How do they make you act or feel?

_____

_____

_____

_____

_____

Why do you fall into these patterns of behavior? What do they do for you (benefit)?

_____

_____

_____

_____

_____

Look at the following list of signs and indicators of **Chaos** and check off the behaviors you identify with now, or in your past:

**Chaos**
- ☐ Negative Thoughts
- ☐ Consumed with fear
- ☐ Super busy or working too much, have to "do it all"
- ☐ Can't relax, can't turn off thoughts
- ☐ Skipping meals or binge eating
- ☐ Excessive exercise or obsessive with habits
- ☐ Judgmental attitude, critical spirit, blaming
- ☐ Overspending or financial stress
- ☐ Lack of sleep or down time
- ☐ No time for family, friends or healthy relationships
- ☐ Avoiding responsibilities
- ☐ Difficulty being alone with people or listening to others

Of these behaviors, what are the one or two most impactful patterns for you?

_____

_____

_____

_____

_____

_____

How do these behaviors affect you? How do they make you act or feel?

_____

_____

_____

_____

Why do you fall into these patterns of behavior? What do they do for you (benefit)?

_____

_____

_____

_____

Look at the following list of signs and indicators of **_Emotional Imbalance_** and check off the behaviors you identify with now, or in your past:

**Emotional Imbalance**
- ☐ Overreactions
- ☐ Defensiveness, rationalizations and justifications
- ☐ Excessive worry, anxiety, fear or nervousness
- ☐ Holding onto resentments, bitterness, anger
- ☐ Replaying old negative thought patterns
- ☐ Argumentative and vengeful
- ☐ Irritable or fits of anger, feeling loss of control
- ☐ Unusually mood swings—outbursts or inward turmoil
- ☐ Affected health from emotional state (stomach aches, headaches, etc.)
- ☐ Can't take feedback or criticism
- ☐ Self pity or victim stance
- ☐ Feeling alone and untrusting of others
- ☐ Avoiding others and feel others are avoiding you

Of these behaviors, what are the one or two most impactful patterns for you?

_____

_____

_____

_____

_____

How do these behaviors affect you? How do they make you act or feel?

_____

_____

_____

_____

Why do you fall into these patterns of behavior? What do they do for you (benefit)?

_____

_____

_____

_____

Look at the following list of signs and indicators of **Burnout** and check off the behaviors you identify with now, or in your past:

**Burnout**
- ☐ Loss of energy or willingness to be active
- ☐ Feeling hopeless or depressed
- ☐ Difficulty concentrating or thinking straight, forgetfulness
- ☐ Increase of confusion or helplessness
- ☐ Feeling overwhelmed
- ☐ Sleeping too much or too little
- ☐ Crying or isolating for no apparent reason
- ☐ Lack of coping with challenges
- ☐ Increased desire to escape or run away
- ☐ Constant cravings for past coping behaviors (alcohol, drugs, food, porn, etc)
- ☐ Fantasizing of good 'ol days
- ☐ Self harm or self abuse
- ☐ Seeking old unhealthy people, places or rituals

Of these behaviors, what are the one or two most impactful patterns for you?

_____

_____

_____

_____

_____

How do these behaviors affect you? How do they make you act or feel?

_____

_____

_____

_____

_____

Why do you fall into these patterns of behavior? What do they do for you (benefit)?

_____

_____

_____

_____

_____

You can see how *losing focus* leads to living in *chaos*, which can then cause *emotional imbalance*. Once you are out of balance emotionally and living in chaos, it is easy to *burnout* and then slip back into survival mode with old coping patterns. You have to be intentional and proactive to stop this slippery slope.

As you can see, there are many indicators and red flags to help us become aware, before we fall into relapse or slip back into old struggles, habits or sinful ways. The key is to become aware of the specific patterns of behavior that you have utilized in the past to make opportunity for temptation and acting out in your struggle.

The biggest help in this process of growth is a good accountability partner. You will need someone to help you see the blind spots and help you become aware when these patterns or indicators are starting in your life. To help with that, you will need to share with your accountability partner your biggest indicators and discuss with them the effect it has on your life and what it looks like when you slip back into those ways. Use the card at the bottom of this sheet to record your biggest issues, and then share it and discuss it with your accountability partner.

--------------------------------------------------------------------------------

Name: _____

(list behavior patterns from each area that you usually fall into)

When I *Lose Focus*: _____

_____

_____

_____

_____


When I fall into *Chaos*: _____

_____

_____

_____

_____


When I become *Emotionally Imbalanced*: _____

_____

_____

_____

_____


When I experience *Burnout*: _____

_____

_____

_____

_____

# THE CHOICE TO CONNECT

*Action 1—Connect with God*

Our first choice towards freedom was surrendering to Christ. That choice was crucial to your eternal life but so is building your relationship with God. When we choose to connect with God and live in relationship with Him, we can experience the lasting freedom we all desire. We can experience the joy, peace and comfort that God offers each moment, all day long.

But let's be honest, connecting with God doesn't just happen on it's own, it will take action on your part. Consider your most important and healthy relationships in life, like your spouse, friends, and family. Do these relationships come easy, or do they take effort to develop, build and maintain?

When you think about a relationship, what would you say are the most important elements?

_____

_____

_____

_____

_____

_____

_____

When you consider your closest relationships, what actions do you take to develop and maintain those important elements of relationship?

_____

_____

_____

_____

_____

_____

The most important relationship that we can have in life is with God. It's not just knowing who God is, but doing life together with him. It's actively developing those most important elements of relationship with Him, the same way we do with others in our life.

Since you have began you journey to freedom, how has your description of God changed? What have you learned about whom He is and His characteristics?

_____

_____

_____

_____

_____

_____

One very important characteristic of healthy relationships is trust. You must have trust in the other person if you are going to move forward together. If there isn't trust, then you will constantly be insecure with the person and the relationship will suffer. The same is true when it comes to God. I believe this is one of the biggest reasons why people push God aside. They do not trust God.

How do you develop trust in your relationships?

_____

_____

_____

_____

_____

_____

In the Merriam-Webster dictionary, it says that trust is the assured reliance on the character, ability, strength, or truth of someone. How can you develop trust in the character, ability, strength and truth of God?

_____

_____

_____

_____

_____

_____

Another very important characteristic of healthy relationships is honesty. There can never be trust in a relationship where one is not honest with the other. What holds you back from being honest with God?

_____

_____

_____

_____

_____

_____

Whatever you are struggling with, you need someone that is completely reliable and trustworthy on your side. Someone you can be honest with and trust they have your best interest. You need someone who understands what you are facing and has the ability to help you with unlimited resources. God is the only person like that. This is why you need to trust and build a relationship with Him.

In Proverbs 3:5-6, it says, *"Trust in the Lord with all your heart and lean not on your own understanding; in all your ways submit to him, and he will make your paths straight."*

What is the promised result if we are honest with God, and trust Him with all your heart?

_____

_____

_____

_____

_____

As you are honest and trust God, you can grow in your relationship with Him each day. You can learn to communicate with Him, be honest with your thoughts and feelings, trust His character and learn more about Him each day. Let me give you a few ideas on how you can do that.

## Daily Prayer

First, we need to start by spending time with God daily. This is not a one and done thing that happens in the morning or before you go to bed. We spend time with him throughout our day. No healthy relationship talks for a brief time in the morning or evening and then is silent for the rest of the day. It is continual conversation. It's making a habit of connection with him. Prayer is communication with God.

Look at the following scriptures and write down the command or encouragement:

Philippians 4:6

_____

_____

_____

_____

_____

_____

Ephesians 6:18

_____

_____

_____

_____

_____

1 Thessalonians 5:16-18

_____

_____

_____

_____

_____

Based on those scriptures, what role does prayer play in growing your relationship with God and developing your connection with Him?

_____

_____

_____

_____

_____

Your prayers will develop a spiritual connection with God through means of thanksgiving, adoration, petition, and confession. The best thing about prayer is that God meets you where you are. He comes alongside you to lead you into a deeper, more intimate relationship with Him, not motivated by guilt, but driven by His love. Prayer changes you. Prayer changes your life.

### Daily Bible Study

Secondly, we need to also spend time reading the bible each day. The bible is our life instruction manual. It tells us how to live, what to do and what to stay away from. The key is developing a consistent habit of reading God's word and learning to understand and apply it to your life. There are many different methods of Bible study, but what is most important is that you do it! You can get a reading plan or start by reading a book (the book of John is a great place to begin), and then journal or write down what it says and how it applies to your life. You can also read a scripture from a devotional or Bible study and answer questions that will help you understand and apply.

Whatever way you choose to study, it is good to read at a comfortable pace and ask yourself:

- Who wrote the book?
- Who is it written to?
- What is the context of the message?
- What can you take away or apply to your life?

If you find that you don't understand something, write it down and ask your accountability partner or a pastor.

Look at the following scriptures and write down the importance of God's word:

2 Timothy 3:16-17

_____

_____

_____

_____

_____

Hebrews 4:12

_____

_____

_____

_____

Proverbs 30:5

_____

_____

_____

_____

Based on the scriptures, how will the studying of God's word be important to developing character?

_____

_____

_____

_____

Daily Bible reading and studying of God's word is instrumental in your ability to understand God's will and His plan and purpose for you. His word is the truth we can trust and follow, and God will reveal Himself to us through His word. Jeremiah 29:13 says, **"You** *will seek me and find me when you search for me with all your heart.* " God desires for you to know Him and walk with Him through His word.

### Bible Scripture Memorization

Another great spiritual discipline that will help you grow in your relationship with God is to not only read God's word, but to memorize scriptures. You do not have to memorize whole passages or try to master the whole Bible. But, getting key scriptures that really speak to you, encourage you and instruct you in life can be very satisfying and strengthen your faith.

Look at the following scriptures and write down the importance of memorizing scriptures:

Psalm 119:11

_____

_____

_____

_____

_____

Joshua 1:8

_____

_____

_____

_____

_____

Psalm 1:2

_____

_____

_____

_____

_____

Based on the scriptures, how will memorizing scripture be important to developing your relationship with God and your daily walk?

_____

_____

_____

_____

_____

_____

_____

_____

_____

Memorizing scripture is key to reinforcing the truth of God's word, and combatting the lies from the enemy. Just like Jesus used scripture to defend against the temptations of the enemy (Matthew 4:1-10), you will need God's word ready to fight off temptations to go back your former habits and destructive patterns.

What is one thing that you can do this week that will help you connect with God better? Be specific

_____

_____

_____

_____

_____

_____

_____

_____

_____

The more that we connect with God, the more we will stay on the right path. He needs to be the most important relationship that we have. He will give us wisdom and direction. He will be there to comfort and protect us. He is the one that no matter what we do, will be there for us. Your choice to connect must start with God and then we move forward.

# THE CHOICE TO CONNECT

*Action 2—Connect with Others*

As we continue the journey toward freedom, you will not only need a relationship with God, but also others. You will need to connect with and develop healthy relationships with other people who will help you, support you and even those you may be able to help and encourage too.

Trying to change and experience freedom on our own is often the one thing that holds us back from moving forward. There is a common temptation to work harder and not include others in the process, but that doesn't usually lead to freedom. We really need other people to help us in this process. But it's important to connect with the right people. It will become important for you to learn the difference between healthy and unhealthy people in your life.

What are the 3 or 4 most important characteristics you are looking for in a healthy relationship?

_____

_____

_____

_____

_____

_____

_____

What are some unhealthy characteristics you have experienced in relationships?

_____

_____

_____

_____

_____

_____

We are all attracted to certain types of people. Often, we choose them and don't really consider the effect they will have on us. There may be many different reasons you are drawn to unhealthy people (insecurity, unmet needs, codependency). But it is not often that you seek out unhealthy people on purpose. Rather, you move into relationship and end up getting hurt because you didn't consider the toxic qualities or characteristics.

Have you had a relationship with someone who may possess the following qualities? And what was the result or hurt from that relationship?

**Controlling**

_____

_____

_____

_____

_____

**Negative/Critical**

_____

_____

_____

_____

_____

**Judgmental**

_____

_____

_____

_____

These types of people often end up using you, hurting you and bringing you down. Sometimes we don't even recognize how unhealthy they are until it becomes an abusive relationship. The reason that this happens points back to your own unmet needs. You might be looking for someone to meet a need in yourself that they cannot, and weren't designed to meet. In fact, when we seek out these unhealthy relationships, they can impact your own character negatively.

1 Corinthians 15:33 says, ***"Do not be deceived: "Bad company corrupts good character."*** If you want to experience freedom, you will want to avoid toxic relationships, and seek to find healthy ones.

As you look to find and connect with healthy people, consider the following scripture from Ecclesiastes 4:9-12:

> *"Two are better than one, because they have a good return for their labor: If either of them falls down, one can help the other up. But pity anyone who falls and has no one to help them up. Also, if two lie down together, they will keep warm. But how can one keep warm alone? Though one may be overpowered, two can defend themselves. A cord of three strands is not quickly broken."*

What does this scripture teach you about relationships?

_____
_____
_____
_____
_____

Have you ever had relationships with the following characteristics? If so, who was it and what was the result or effect upon you?

**Supportive**

_____
_____
_____
_____
_____

**Encouragement**

_____

_____

_____

_____

_____

**Respectful**

_____

_____

_____

_____

_____

**Honest**

_____

_____

_____

_____

_____

**Trustworthy**

_____

_____

_____

_____

_____

These five characteristics are important as you look to connect and develop healthy relationships with others. It may seem overwhelming to pursue a relationship like this but it is worth it. People are the main reason that we get hurt and people are what we need to be healed.

Who do you have in your life right now that is healthy and supportive?

1. _____

2. _____

3. _____

If you don't have healthy and supportive relationships in your life, then you may want to start reaching out and finding someone like that. You will need to be proactive because the person is not going to find you. A good place to start is in a church, your recovery group, small group or a community group. We need to put ourselves in environments with people, even if it is difficult.

During this journey to freedom, it is wise to start seeking out healthy relationships and building your support team or network to help you move forward with your life changes. There are several intentional relationships that are important for this process; a mentor, several teammates, and someone to give back to.

## Mentor

A mentor is someone who has walked the road ahead of you and has gained experience, wisdom and insight, and is willing to walk beside you in your journey of life change. They are a great person to talk to and provide supportive, objective, and honest feedback. They can encourage you from a place of understanding, because they have been in your shoes or have walked a similar journey you are embarking on. Most important, they can demonstrate and model a healthy, Christian lifestyle that can be inspiring and helpful to you.

A mentor can be found in your Freedom Group, but may also be outside your group. They may be someone you know in your church community, or your professional community, that you admire, respect or see how they can benefit you in this life change process.

Proverbs 20:5 says, *though good advice lies deep within the heart, a person with understanding will draw it out.*" This is exactly what a good mentor can do for you.

Who can you think of, that might be a good mentor? (possibly more than one person)

_____

_____

_____

_____

_____

How would a mentor be helpful for you?

_____

_____

_____

_____

_____

## Teammate

If you consider a mentor someone who has walked the road ahead of you, then a teammate would be someone who is also walking this road with you and fighting the daily battle with you. Just like a teammate on a sports team, you can form a partnership to help each other. You will need several teammates to walk the journey to life change together with you. These are people who can relate to your struggles, hold you accountable, provide mutual encouragement, and are going through the same process you are—even if their specific struggle or habit may be different.

Most often, these are people from your Freedom Group, or small group, or church community group. Hopefully, you can find several partners to walk this road with you. It will be your responsibility to reach out to them consistently and build the supportive relationship, as they will sometimes need your help, just like you will need their help.

Who can you ask to walk with you as a teammate in your life change process?

_____

_____

_____

_____

_____

Take the time this next week to talk a few possible teammates and start building your team. Often, these people are the ones that make the journey the most fun, and can become some of your best friends and support during hard times.

The third type of person is someone you can give back to, and can intentionally help. We will discuss this relationship more in the next Action step.

# THE CHOICE TO CONNECT

*Action 3—Give Back to Others*

As you connect with others in this process of life change, you will start to grow and learn. You can actually become a person who can provide wisdom and insight from your own experience.

When you are hurting or struggling in life the focus is only on you. That is not a bad thing because you need to focus on getting healthy. But there comes a time where you need to take the focus off of yourself and place the focus on others. In fact, when we reach out to others, it can bring us healing and health. As you walk through the process of recovery, it will go both ways; you can receive, but you must give as well.

How do you feel about possibly helping others who may be struggling?

_____

_____

_____

_____

_____

What could be an obstacle to finding others you could give back to and help?

_____

_____

_____

_____

_____

Read Luke 6:38. What does the Bible teach about giving back to others through this passage?

_____

_____

_____

_____

_____

It is clear that if you give to others, it will be given back to you. The amount you give will determine the amount you get back. We cannot out give God and He wants us to give to one another because it will not only help someone but it will benefit us greatly.

In fact, your experience and what have you have learned in this journey to freedom is unique to you. But in that uniqueness, there is so much that can be shared and useful for others. Just think, right now there may be someone in your world who is need of what you can uniquely give!

What have you learned that can be shared with someone else?

_____

_____

_____

_____

_____

How can you share what you have learned or experienced in this Freedom Group process?

_____

_____

_____

_____

When we talk about giving back, it doesn't always mean you will give out of your process of life change. It also applies to God creating a generous spirit within you that desires to be shared with others. God has given you unique talents, interests and experiences that can be shared with others, in a way that brings God honor.

We all have things to give. God has given us all unique gifts and talents. What you can give another person is not what the next person can give. This is what makes us unique and equally beneficial.

Think about the following gifts and talents and how they could be used to help someone else:

- Encourager
- Helper
- Musical
- Organized
- Artistic
- Physical Strength
- Teaching
- Compassion
- Kindness
- Listening
- Financially Sound

Every one of these gifts, and many more, can be effective ways to help someone else that may be in need. Sometimes we think that we have to do something really big in order to give to others but God just wants us to give what we have.

What characteristics or personality traits do you possess, that can be used to help other people?

_____
_____
_____
_____
_____
_____
_____

If you can be willing to share what you have been given, God will use it to make a difference in the lives of other people. Something amazing happens when you get outside of yourself and focus on others, and use your gifts and talents to be a blessing and help someone else.

Where can you find opportunities to help and share your gifts?

_____

_____

_____

_____

_____

What is something you can this next week to help someone else? How can you start giving back to others?

_____

_____

_____

_____

_____

You can make a difference if you choose to give back to others. When you do that, you are trading selfishness for selflessness. It's amazing how good you can feel when you reach out to others.

# THE CHOICE TO CONNECT

*Action 4—Share Your Testimony*

Everyone has a story. Maybe you have heard this phrase before, but it is very true. No one in the world has the same story that you have. Everyone you lock eyes with at the store or at your workplace, has a unique story of their lives. Each person's story has had struggles and victories, and each one has had its ups and downs.

There is power and healing in the telling of your story. Often, the things in life that are the most painful can be utilized as great strengths. In sharing your story with others, there is the potential for connection and positive impact. When you know that someone understands what you have gone through, there is a natural connection. That is why your story, and your journey of healing and growth, and the experience you have had finding true freedom, is so very important.

What are some things you have learned about yourself and experienced during this Freedom Group that can be beneficial and impactful for others?

_____

_____

_____

_____

_____

_____

1 Peter 3:15 says, *"Always be prepared to give an answer to everyone who asks you to give the reason for the hope that you have."*

Matthew 5:15 says, *"No one lights a lamp and then puts it under a basket. Instead, a lamp is placed on a stand, where it gives light to everyone in the house."*

As people start to see the changes in your life, you need to be prepared to share your story, and share the hope you have gained through Jesus. The impact of your changes is not meant to stay hidden or kept to yourself. God wants to use your story to impact others.

Fear often keeps you and others from reaching out and getting the needed help, or making the necessary changes in life. One of the things that breaks that fear is when someone meets another person that has struggled with the same thing. Your story can be the catalyst for breaking someone's fear and helping them get help and make their own life changes.

What fear do you have about sharing your story?

_____

_____

_____

_____

_____

Have you ever been impacted by hearing someone else's story? How did that help you?

_____

_____

_____

_____

_____

Your story is uniquely yours, with unique experiences. We call this a testimony. As a Christ follower, your testimony is sharing how Jesus changed our life.

Think about dividing your life into three sections. The first is what your life was like before Christ. In many cases, this is explaining your life that may have been hopeless without Christ. You may have struggled with addictions, destructive habits or negative experiences.

Next, share how we came to accept Christ. For some of you, that may have happened in this Freedom Group, during this journey to finding freedom. For others, this may have happened a long time ago, and your life just got off track, or struggled after that decision.

The last part of our testimony is sharing what has happened after we have asked Christ to come into our lives and the future He has for us now. This is the positive experience you may be feeling now, since you have worked to overcome the struggles and habits, and are set to live a life a freedom.

Let's take some time now to write your testimony. Take a few moments to stop and pray, and ask God to help you share honestly and courageously. There may be fears or other obstacles to honestly sharing your story. But with God by your side, you can be brave, open, honest and transparent in telling your story.

For each of the three sections, there will be some questions or prompts to help you get started. Take the time to consider them and then write your response in story form in the space provided.

## 1. Life before Christ
- What was your life like before you accepted Christ?
- What were words or feelings to describe your life before Christ?
- What was your relationship with God like, if you even had a relationship?
- What was your attitude towards others?
- What was your lowest point, or rock bottom moment?

_____

_____

_____

_____

_____

_____

_____

_____

_____

_____

_____

_____

_____

_____

_____

**2. How did you come to accept Christ?**
- What brought you to the place of needing help?
- How did you reach out for help?
- How did God reveal himself to you?
- How did you come to the decision to accept Christ?
- What did it feel like to make that decision, and what are the words to describe your experience accepting Christ?

_____

_____

_____

_____

_____

_____

_____

_____

_____

_____

_____

**3. What is your future like with Christ in your life?**
- What has changed since Christ has come into your life?
- How has it affected your relationships with others?
- What has God shown you that can help others?
- What does your life feel like now with Christ leading?
- Do you want to help others?
- What are your passions and dreams for the future?

_____

_____

_____

_____

_____

_____

_____

_____

_____

There is such power in the sharing of your story. A couple of times a year, we schedule several people to share their testimony at our church gathering. It almost always becomes one of our most talked about services. Why is that? Because people connect with personal stories of life change. We tell each person or couple that they have between three and five minutes to share. It seems like a very short time but you would be surprised on the power of their short story.

You should be prepared to tell your short story, in only three to five minutes. As you share your story with someone, you may provide the key to unlocking his or her pain. You never know the difference that you can make.

Who can you share your story with? Is there anybody you can tell, just to practice telling your story?

_____

_____

_____

_____

_____

# ABOUT THE AUTHOR

 Landon Porter is a Pastor with a heart for helping people find and experience Freedom and life change through authentic relationships with each other and God. He has more than 13 years personal experience in recovery and life transformation and has spent 12 years leading others to freedom from addictions and destructive habits. He currently serves as a Groups Pastor at Northview Church in Carmel, Indiana. Previously, Landon served as the Care & Recovery Groups Pastor at Sagebrush Church in Albuquerque, New Mexico where he helped lead the dynamic Living Free ministry. He has written several group curriculums used in the Living Free recovery groups and has developed leadership training for recovery groups. Landon and his wife Stephanie, regularly speak on topics related to marriage and recovery, and have recently launched their ministry, Authentic Marriage. He earned a B.S in Education from Abilene Christian University, and an M.S. in Exercise Science and Sports Leadership from Seattle Pacific University. Landon spent 17 years as a High School educator and 12 years as Head Basketball Coach, in several cities including Austin, TX, Lynnwood, WA and Albuquerque, NM.